THE LANGUAGE OF THE MARKET

THE LANGUAGE OF THE MARKET

UNDERSTANDING CHARTS THROUGH PRICE AND VOLUME

DAVID CARMONA RODRÍGUEZ

The Language of the Market: Understanding charts through price and volume.

ISBN: 978-84-09-76740-3

First edition: September 2025

To all those who dedicate part of their savings to investing in search of a more prosperous future.

Special thanks to J.A. Herrera (MarketReader), for generously reviewing the theoretical part of this book.

CONTENTS

PROLOGUE

VSA (Volume Spread Analysis) represents the decoding of the footprint left by professionals in the markets. This methodology, which combines the reading of price and volume, allows us to identify whether institutional players are actively or passively buying or selling, and is considered one of the most reliable tools for operating in financial markets.

Richard Wyckoff was the pioneer of this approach at the beginning of the 20th century. However, the person who truly brought this methodology into the spotlight was Tom Williams, often regarded as the modern father of Wyckoff, especially in the Internet era. Williams used his deep knowledge of price and volume to develop his own software, *TradeGuider*, which helped thousands of traders around the world interpret charts more effectively.

So, why use this methodology? What makes VSA so effective is its ability to offer a genuine, direct, and transparent reading of the market. Through volume, VSA reveals when professionals are acting, giving investors a powerful tool to make informed decisions.

At the same time, within VSA analysis, it is essential to understand the different roles of the market participants.

First, we have the strong hands: large capitalists, investment funds, and syndicates with the financial capacity to influence the market and consistently profit from it. These players are usually the ones who capture the largest gains over time, taking advantage of their ability to strategically and collectively move significant amounts of capital.

On the other side, we find the weak hands, which include the general public, retail traders, and even certain investment funds and banks. Weak hands are usually at a disadvantage compared to strong hands, and more often than not, they end up losing money in the long run, especially when they fail to interpret the moves of professionals.

Finally, there are the market makers, key players in this ecosystem. Their main function is to guarantee liquidity, acting as counterparties at any point in the chart, which ensures that trades can be executed continuously. But their role is not limited to providing liquidity—they also aim to maximize their own profits. Market makers are constantly alert to opportunities that arise in the market, taking advantage of every move that can give them an edge, often in sync with strong hands.

In short, understanding how these participants operate and the signals they leave in the market is what makes VSA such a powerful and effective tool. Identifying the moves of strong hands, avoiding the traps set by market makers, and recognizing the behaviour of weak hands can be the difference between success and failure in the markets.

That's why, for those who are just starting their journey in the stock market, my advice is clear: education is fundamental. Before jumping into trading, it is crucial to understand how to read charts, how to interpret volume, and above all, how to detect the footprint left by professionals.

It must be said that VSA is one of the most confusing tools for beginners. This is because the very same bar, with the same characteristics and volume, can have different implications depending on the context in which it appears.

Only through deep knowledge of the market and tools such as VSA can new traders truly learn to understand the language of the market and avoid the traps that consistently catch weak hands.

Preparation is the only path to success in this complex, yet fascinating, world of financial markets.

J.A. Herrera

The mentor who guided me into the world of VSA

INTRODUCTION

The Language of the Market. That is how I have decided to title this book, which is essentially a compilation of all the stock market notes I have put together over the years.

First of all, I should say that I am not an economist or anything of the sort. Some of you may already know me from my YouTube channel or from X (formerly Twitter), where I go by the name RA8 Finance. RA8 comes from the Spanish 'Real de a ocho', the old currency of the Spanish Empire—a long story. As for me, I'm in my thirties, from Madrid, and a Civil Engineer by training. In other words, nothing to do with the world of finance.

However, my passion for the stock market began when I was eighteen. As you enter adulthood and leave adolescence behind, you start hearing more serious conversations, often about money. I remember one day on the news they said the stock market had fallen sharply and that there were fears of a recession in Europe. From that moment, I became deeply interested in economics, in basic concepts such as inflation, compound interest, and all those things that most Spaniards (unfortunately) find somewhat alien.

Not long after, when I was already of legal age, my father told me he had €3,000 sitting idle in the bank and wanted to invest it. Since I had already been curious about the stock market for a few months, I started looking at options in the Spanish equity market. That was my very first experience with investing—the first stepping stone on my journey.

I had read about both fundamental and technical analysis in various books. Since I wasn't an economist, fundamental analysis seemed too difficult, requiring too much time and effort to understand concepts that weren't exactly simple for me at that stage. So, I decided to dive into the fascinating world of technical analysis.

What could I do with €3,000? Which stocks could I buy?

Before investing, I read a pile of classic technical analysis books, where I "learned" how to interpret the market: channels, trend lines, head-and-shoulders patterns, double tops, and, above all, countless indicators (MACD, RSI, stochastic, moving averages, etc.). I downloaded *ProRealTime* onto my laptop and began analysing IBEX-35 charts.

After a few weeks scanning the market, I told my father he should invest the money in Grifols, Banco Santander, and Repsol, as they looked promising. However, he told me to do it myself through the bank's broker. And so, I did: I opened a securities account and placed my very first stock market trade.

"Unfortunately," the shares went up and I sold shortly after, making a profit. This is brilliant! That feeling of making money without having to go to an office, just by looking at charts with indicators and trend lines, felt like an amazing discovery. So, with the profits, I carried on trading. Looking back, I still don't know how I managed to go on winning and losing trades for at least three years and still stay in the green.

But eventually, the trade sizes grew larger, and risk management began to slip out of my control. I wanted to be more ambitious, now with a fair amount of experience under my belt. The problem was that every time I invested in a stock, I became far too obsessed with its daily fluctuations. Continuous stress. How can the price be falling if there's been a bullish crossover in the MACD and the RSI is oversold?

Then came the pandemic. By sheer luck, the crash of early 2020 didn't catch me in the market. But there was one stock firmly on my radar: IAG.

With flights grounded worldwide, airline shares had collapsed. I thought it was the perfect time to buy. The stock had dropped more than 60%, so I decided to purchase a significant position. All the indicators pointed to oversold conditions, so it seemed only a matter of time before a strong rebound.

But the worst was yet to come. The price stabilised for a while, only to drop another 50%. By then I was using stop-losses, but not in that trade. To make matters worse, the company announced a highly dilutive capital increase. As I had no extra money to participate, my shares were diluted, and the value of my investment was shattered.

That trade wiped out years of progress in the stock market, leaving me deep in the red. I decided to sell at a 65% loss. Weeks later, after the capital increase, the Covid-19 vaccine was announced and the stock jumped 150% in just a few weeks. You can imagine my face—utter disbelief and frustration.

From today's perspective, that trade was actually a blessing. A game changer, as the English call it: an event that shifts the course of things. I realised it was time to stop and reflect. Was it really profitable to carry on with the same strategy? Were my analyses, based on mathematical indicators, truly effective? After much thought, I stumbled upon a different approach to technical analysis.

In November 2020, through social media, I discovered a book that focused on analysing market movements using only price and volume. Volume was something I always had on my charts but had never paid much attention to. From the moment I read that book by Miguel Ramírez (see Bibliography), my outlook on the market completely changed.

I spent years studying this methodology in depth and testing it in practice. I also expanded my knowledge of risk management during that time, always using stop-losses in my trades. The combination of both was the key to understanding and operating in the market with the lowest possible risk.

I documented everything in notes. Later, I met my mentor, known on social media as Market Reader, and I was able to deepen my understanding of all the concepts of VSA. Bar by bar, I began to see the meaning behind market movements. With hard work and countless hours observing charts, I gradually came to understand why certain moves occur and how to take advantage of them.

Day by day, I continue learning new things about the market—and that is what excites me the most. That's why I gathered all my VSA notes and decided to publish this book. It is essentially a study guide, full of concepts that need to be practised in order to be fully understood. That is why I chose a practical approach, with numerous examples and charts to make everything as didactic and engaging as possible.

If you are looking here for secret rules or magic formulas to get rich, you can stop reading now. That is not what this book is about. There are no shortcuts to overnight wealth here, only keys to understanding the language of the market through VSA. I hope that point is clear enough.

As for the structure of the book:

The first part covers the most basic concepts of price and volume.

The second part goes deep into the VSA methodology, with a detailed explanation of all the market bars and the main structures that appear again and again in every asset and timeframe.

The third part gives a brief overview of Elliott Wave Theory, which seeks to structure market movements. There are many books on this subject, so I have not sought to replicate what is already out there, but rather to highlight what I consider essential.

Finally, my favourite chapter: the case studies. This section contains twenty real-life market examples—the very thing I always wished I had when I first started studying price and volume methodology: real, practical examples.

Without further ado, I hope you enjoy this book as much as I have enjoyed writing it.

A Note to the Reader

This book is a translation of the original work in Spanish, 'El Lenguaje del Mercado' published in December 2024. While every effort has been made to ensure accuracy, there may be some minor errors or ambiguities in the English translation, particularly in the chart labels. Please rest assured that these do not in any way impact the core ideas and concepts conveyed throughout the text.

1. FIRST STEPS

If you are reading this book, it is because you are interested in learning about the methodology that decodes the market through price and volume.

Whether you are already an expert in the field or have no idea what's coming, it is important that, before diving in, we first go over some basic concepts of financial markets.

1.1 THE MARKET AND THE MAIN PLAYERS

We are about to enter the fascinating world of the stock market, commonly referred to as equities. It is called variable income in Spanish because the return is not fixed or guaranteed but varies depending on many factors. Since this is not a conventional stock market textbook, I won't go into detail about the technicalities of the different investment instruments currently available to the public.

What we must be clear about is that in the stock market we are up against the best players on the planet: those with the most money, the sharpest minds from the best universities, and those who truly profit from this business. We will call all of them professionals—or strong hands.

Unlike, say, civil engineering, which requires a degree and a professional licence to practise, in the stock market anyone with an internet connection and a brokerage account can participate.

However, you should know that if you do not understand how the market works, chances are you will lose everything at the very beginning.

And here, what is at risk is your money, the money you worked so hard to earn. You have dedicated part of your life to making that money, only to risk losing it in the market. Because yes, in the stock market you can lose all your money, and even more, depending on the investment product you choose. That's why it's best to come prepared, with at least some basic knowledge, before investing.

This is why we distinguish between strong hands and weak hands in the market.

Tom Williams explains this very well in his book Master the Markets (essential reading before you start trading). He says that "strong hands are strong precisely because they are on the right side of the market", while "weak hands are inexperienced traders who tend to make decisions instinctively".

Since strong hands are the true specialists, they tend to take advantage of weak hands when executing their moves. They have no mercy—they are out to take your money. They don't care whether it took you years to earn it, or whether you have three children to support. Their goal is simply to offload shares onto you when they think the market is about to fall, or to take them from you when they believe prices are about to rise.

It is important to highlight that no one controls share prices. All participants take advantage of price fluctuations, but none of them knows with certainty where the market will go next.

Then we have the market makers. They are one of the least understood actors in the market but play a fundamental role in keeping prices stable by ensuring that all orders have a counterparty. In practice, they are entities appointed to guarantee liquidity and reduce excessive fluctuations in listed securities. They are obliged to quote both a bid and an ask price, thus improving market efficiency. And, of course, they also seek to profit along the way—often by sweeping certain liquidity levels before initiating a countertrend move.

If we put strong hands and weak hands together, it's clear which side we should try to follow. Since we don't have the financial firepower of strong hands, the only thing we can do is observe the traces they leave in the market and try to mimic them.

Those traces are what we must learn to follow—and to do so, we need to understand two key concepts: price and volume.

1.2 PRICE AND VOLUME

These two concepts will guide the way we understand the market from now on. Forget about mathematical indicators and intangible tools. Only price and volume. As simple—and at the same time as complex—as to justify countless books written on both.

The price of an asset is governed by the law of supply and demand. You've probably heard that phrase before, and yes, it applies perfectly to the stock market.

To bring it into everyday life: imagine you want to buy a flat (demand) in a neighbourhood. First, you look at all the flats on offer in that area (supply). Once you identify the one you want, there is a negotiation between buyer and seller to set a fair exchange price for the property. When both parties agree, the deal is closed. In short, price is nothing more than the figure at which buyer (demand) and seller (supply) agree to exchange an underlying asset (the flat).

In the stock market, the underlying asset could be a company's share, where the price is again set by supply and demand.

The challenge is that it is not just one buyer or seller, but thousands of them. And it is precisely those countless interactions that move the price of a share up and down.

So, the price of an asset rises for two reasons:

- Demand absorbs most of the supply available in the market.
- There is no supply willing to sell at current market prices.

And, conversely, the price of an asset falls for two reasons:

- Supply exceeds demand.
- There is no demand willing to buy at current market prices.

If we understand all of this and what it implies, then we already have half the book read. The other half begins here.

Earlier we said there are two concepts we must master: price and the law of supply and demand. Up to this point, we've had a glimpse of price. But on its own, price cannot tell us whether supply or demand is prevailing in the market. That's where volume comes in.

Volume represents the number of contracts traded over a given period. If there is high volume in a given timeframe, we can infer that a large number of contracts have changed hands. Conversely, if volume is low, it means market participants are barely active.

Both price and volume are the footprints we must follow in the market. They are represented in charts: the horizontal axis shows time, while the vertical axis shows the asset price.

There are many ways to display price: candlesticks, line charts, point-and-figure charts, or bar charts. In this book, we'll use the classic approach: the bar chart.

As for volume, it will be represented as a histogram, where the height of each bar shows the number of contracts traded in that period.

Chart 1 on the next page is a clear example of what we've just explained.

At the bottom we see volume, and above it, the asset's price. On the x-axis, time (in this case, each segment represents two weeks); on the y-axis, the asset's price (in logarithmic scale).

We will always use logarithmic scales in charts, because moving from $1 to $2 is not the same as moving from $60,001 to $60,002. I'll leave that with you to reflect on.

Chart 1: Bar chart

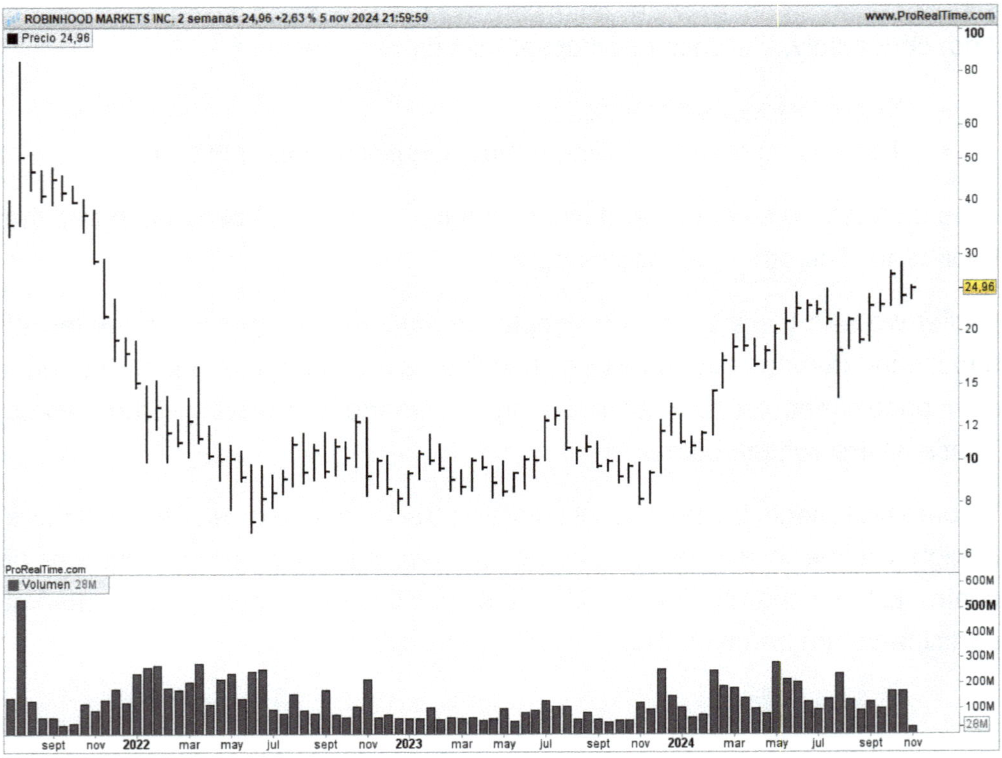

As I mentioned earlier, there are thousands of technical analysis books on how to represent price on a chart. Here, I will briefly stop to describe what a single bar is, like those we saw in the previous chart, so that nothing is left uncovered.

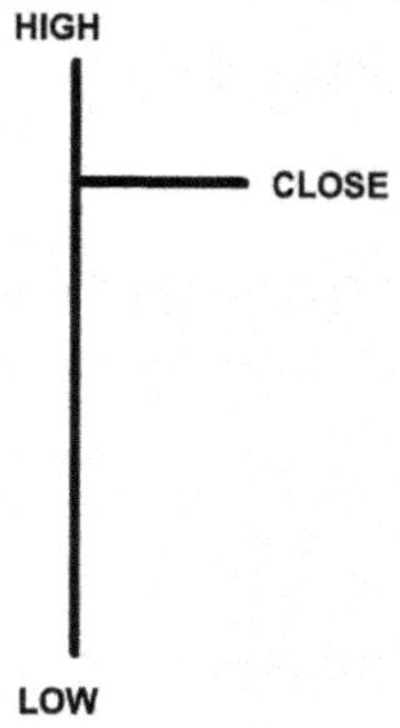

On the left, you can see, in large format, what a price bar is. This bar reflects only three concepts:

High: in the given period of the bar, this is the highest price reached.

Low: in the given period of the bar, this is the lowest price reached.

Close: in the given period of the bar, this is the price at which the bar closed.

Thus, if the close of one bar is higher than the close of the previous bar, we have a bullish movement. If the close of one bar is lower than the close of the previous bar, we have a bearish movement. Simple.

So far, the subject seems easy enough, which is why we are now going to make it a little more complex.

1.3 COMBINING PRICE AND VOLUME

Once we have understood the concepts of price and volume, let's see how they work together. Up until now, we have learnt what are essentially the letters of the alphabet: price and volume. It is a very limited alphabet, as you have already seen. Now we are going back to school and will combine all the letters to form words and learn to communicate.

When you learn a language (and I hope you will confirm this to me once you finish the book), the goal is to speak and understand what the other person is trying to convey.

In the case of the stock market, we are not trying to speak to the market, but rather to understand what it is transmitting to us. To do so, we need to analyse the price and volume charts together. It is like a melody: if you only pay attention to one note, you will never grasp the entire symphony.

Let's go back to the previous chart (Chart 1).

Here we can observe a series of daily bars with their volume. On their own, a single bar tells us very little, but if we place it in context, together they give us a much more complete picture of what is happening in the market.

In this case, we can see that the price first shows a downward trend. Most closes are lower than the closes of the previous bars, and therefore the price falls. We could say that we already know enough to understand that supply has taken control.

Afterwards, the price moves sideways for a while, meaning that supply and demand balance out, and then it rises again, with demand regaining control over supply.

Now, the first thing you need to do is open a charting platform. I use ProRealTime (and no, this is not a sponsored mention), but there are many other platforms that do the same job, such as TradingView, Visual Chart, or the charting tool at Investing.com, among others.

If you take a moment to look at the sea of bars and volumes, you will see that there are many options for viewing charts across different timeframes (each bar can represent a month, a week, a day, an hour, a minute, or even seconds).

Do you need to know all of these timeframes to read the market? Luckily not, because one of the properties of the market is that it repeats itself across different timeframes. This means that price movements occur in the same way on different timeframes. Therefore, the reading of different charts across different timeframes is the same.

However, you must always keep in mind that higher timeframes are much more important than lower timeframes, since they encompass all of them, as in Russian dolls. We will come back to this later.

As I said earlier, this is not a technical analysis textbook, so we are not going to delve into more “drawing” concepts, which you can already find in countless other works. Still, it is worth pausing for a moment on the following concepts.

1.3.1 SUPPORTS, RESISTANCES AND TRENDLINES

If you took a moment to observe the previous chart, you may have noticed that certain price levels or zones are often respected by bars to near perfection. If they don't manage to break through, they bounce back and are rejected again.

Support and resistance are essential concepts in technical analysis. In a downtrend, support acts as a "floor" that prevents further declines, while in an uptrend, resistance serves as a "ceiling" that limits price increases.

These levels can be horizontal or dynamic. Dynamic levels are called trendlines, as they connect successive highs and lows when the price moves within a trend, outlining its direction over time.

When the price respects both an upper and a lower trendline, it forms a channel, either upward or downward, which helps visualise the strength and path of the trend.

As shown in Chart 2, these supports, resistances, and trendlines can be clearly identified in the price action.

Chart 2: Supports, resistances and trendlines.

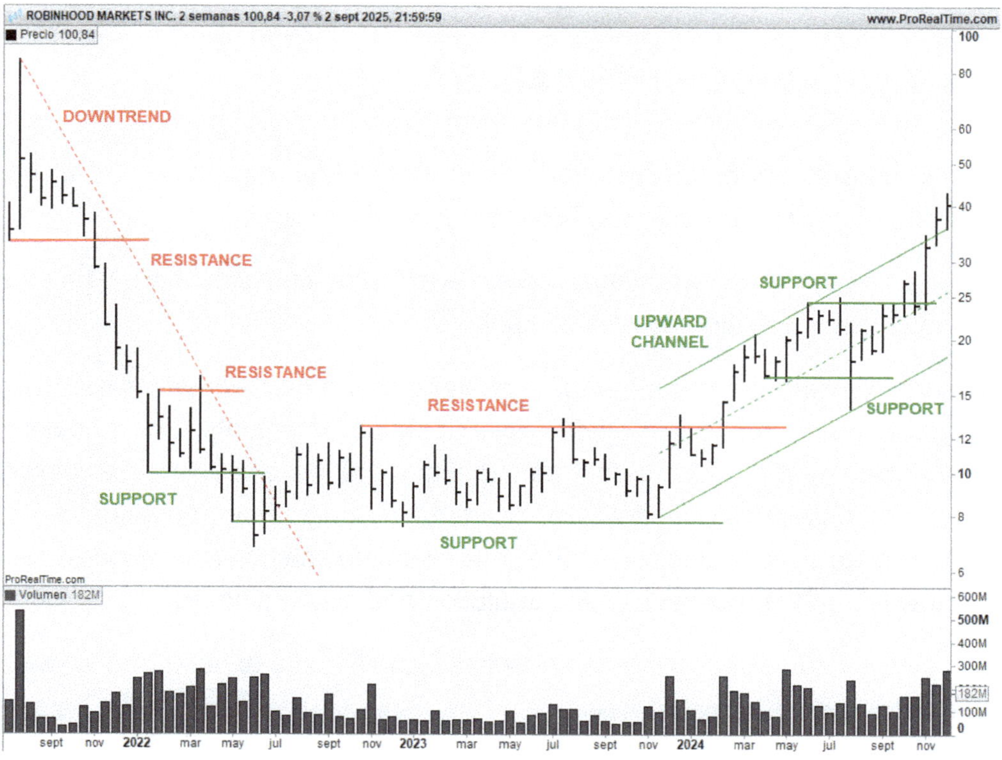

We start with a clear downtrend, where the price breaks supports and turns them into resistances, all guided by a trendline or downward guideline. Then the price breaks the downward guideline, finds a floor, and consolidates sideways, meaning it enters a horizontal range between a support and a resistance.

Eventually, the price breaks the resistance (now turned into support) and enters an upward trend, structuring the impulse within an upward channel, where the lows and highs are connected.

Notice that the last level broken by price was a resistance, but it is labelled as support. This happens because one of the properties of these levels is that when resistance is broken, it immediately becomes support, and vice versa. That is why, in the chart, that level, which was resistance before, now acts as support.

Now all that remains is for you to practise in front of the screen and identify all the supports, resistances, and trendlines that appear in a chart.

The more trained your eye becomes at detecting these levels, the easier it will be to follow the rest of the book.

1.4 THE LAWS OF THE MARKET

A little more theory before we move on to more visual concepts. And along the way, let me introduce you to Richard Wyckoff and VSA.

Who is this gentleman that has appeared for the first time here? (In the prologue there was already a small spoiler).

Richard Wyckoff was one of the first analysts of the markets under the VSA (Volume Spread Analysis) methodology. To put him into context, he was born in 1873 and died in 1934. In that period, when today's charting tools did not exist, he pioneered the analysis of charts using only price and volume. He focused on understanding why share prices went up and down and discovered that it was due to processes of accumulation and distribution.

Do you remember strong hands and weak hands? Let's expand on that with Wyckoff's work.

According to him, prices rise because there has first been an accumulation process by the strong hands, who buy up all the shares from the weak hands. In other words, demand is greater than supply.

Afterwards, an upward trend develops until a point is reached when the strong hands begin to sell shares to the weak hands. In other words, supply is greater than demand.

Thus begins a distribution process which is followed by a downward trend.

A full cycle, as can be seen in Chart 3.

Chart 3: Accumulation and distribution structures

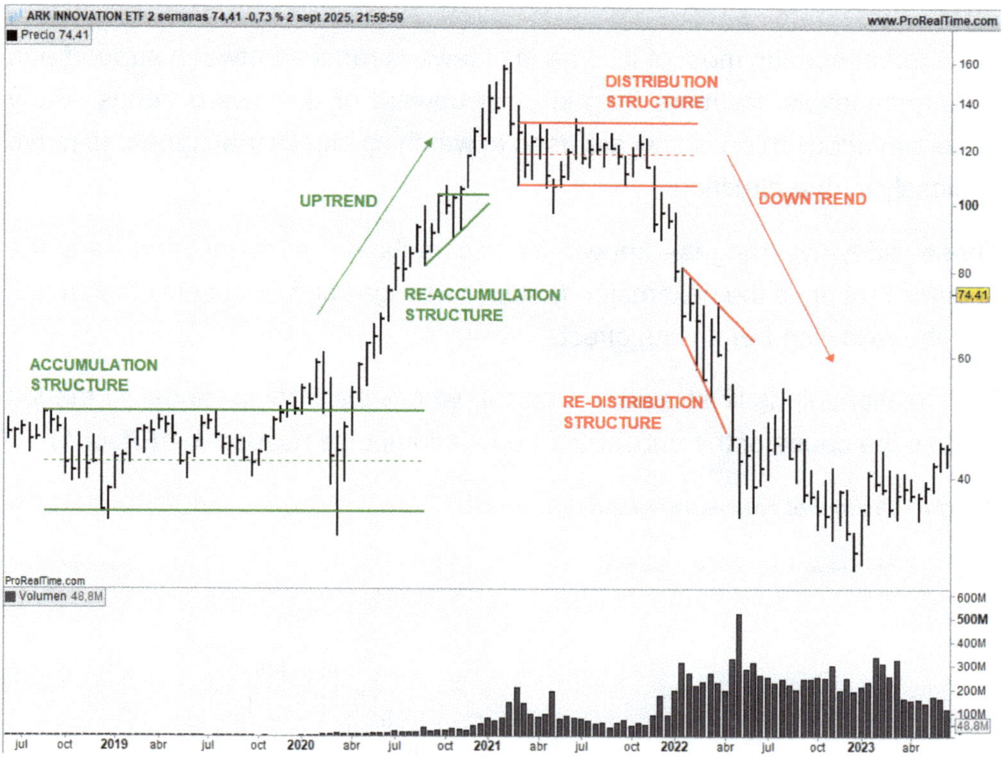

If we add to this the combination of price and volume and their study, Wyckoff created a methodology that was unique in its time. A methodology called VSA, which attempts to read the market.

And did you think I was going to tell you something new in this book? Not at all — this is more than a hundred years old and still just as relevant today!

Wyckoff put forward three fundamental laws that anyone who wants to learn to read the market must know or at least be aware of.

1.4.1 THE LAW OF SUPPLY AND DEMAND

We already know this one, don't we? The market is governed by the law of supply and demand.

In section "1.2 Price and Volume" we already talked about it, so we won't repeat it here.

1.4.2 THE LAW OF CAUSE-AND-EFFECT

The market spends most of its time in sideways ranges between support and resistance levels, far more than in clear upward or downward trends. Many traders overlook this, as they are used to watching stocks that appear to move endlessly in one direction.

These sideways ranges—known as accumulation or distribution—are the engines that drive the next major move. The range itself represents the cause, and the following trend is its effect.

This relationship is illustrated in Chart 4, where the trading range on the left acts as the cause of the subsequent upward impulse (Cause 1 – Effect 1).

Chart 4: The law of cause-and-effect

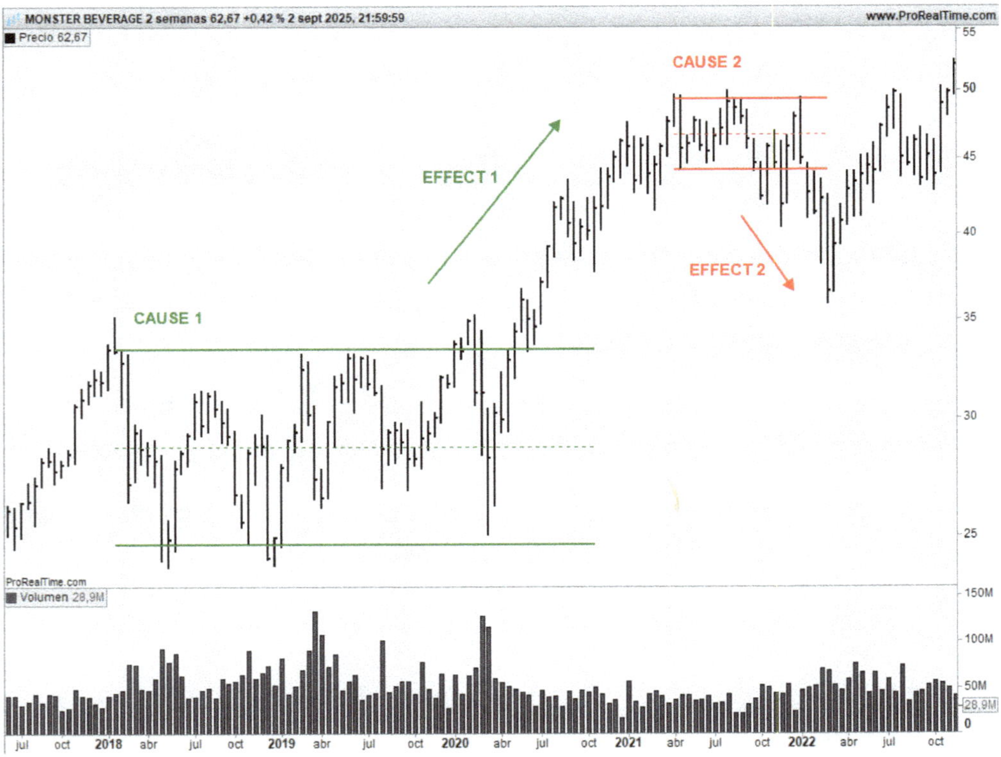

The same happens with the sideways range on the right. In this case, the cause triggered a downward impulse after the break of the lower boundary of the range (Cause 2 – Effect 2).

1.4.3 THE LAW OF EFFORT VS RESULT

If that price range takes little time to form, we could say that the later effect (the subsequent trend) should be proportional to such effort. If, on the other hand, the price range takes a long time to form and the distance between support and resistance is wide, the later effect should be proportional to that range, in other words, it should cover a large distance.

A practical example would be the previous chart (Chart 4). In Cause 1, the range has taken a long time to form and the distance between the lower and upper boundaries is relatively large. Therefore, the effect is proportional and extensive.

In contrast, the range in Cause 2 is narrow and has taken little time to form, so the subsequent effect is limited and of short duration, proportional to its 'cause'.

1.4.4 BEFORE STARTING WORK

In my view, once these basic market concepts have been assimilated, you can start practising many exercises in front of the screen. Personally, that is how I began: by observing and analysing numerous charts over many years.

In them, I suggest identifying all the supports, resistances, ranges, trendlines and channels that you can spot. Practise this across different timeframes and you will see that these levels are respected in both monthly and hourly charts. It is as if price had a memory.

Once you have identified the key levels, look for the trading ranges (the ranges where price moves between a support and a resistance) and draw the trendlines and channels of the subsequent movements.

This is the first step you should take when analysing a chart: key levels, ranges and trendlines. However, with just this, you will not yet be able to read a chart. You need to know what drives price to move in one direction or another — and that is what I will show you in the next chapter.

Are you ready to understand the market??

2. VSA

Once you are familiar with VSA, which, as you know, is nothing more than reading the market by analysing price and volume and have analysed the basic concepts and laws that govern the market, it is time to delve deeper into the methodology.

VSA (Volume Spread Analysis) requires a detailed study of all the bars that make up a price structure. Along with volume, each bar has a unique connotation which, in conjunction with the other bars surrounding it, gives us clues as to the intentions of the strong hands.

That is the essence of it all. Reading the bars, their volume and all of this taken as a whole to detect traces of the manoeuvres being carried out by the strong hands in the asset in question.

To do this, in this chapter we are going to go from less to more. We already know the concepts of support and resistance, ranges, trend lines and channels. Now, we are going to analyse the bars one by one to see if they contain strength or weakness.

When we talk about strength, it means that the bars and volume indicate that the market is ready to see higher prices. When we talk about weakness, it means that the market is prepared to see lower prices.

Subsequently, we will analyse all the bars as a whole, the complete picture. To do this, Wyckoff provided diagrams and broke down the structures into phases, which is vitally important for seeing the connotations (bullish or bearish) of the structure.

Next, we will analyse the types of structures that can be seen in the market, to sharpen our vision and identify them as quickly as possible.

Finally, a short guide to detecting market floors or ceilings.

We will get into technicalities; it is inevitable. However, there will be numerous practical examples to reinforce the theory.

2.1 THE EIGTH STRENGTH BARS

Before getting into the subject, it is necessary to understand the following concepts:

- **Up-bar**: a bar whose closing price is above the closing price of the previous bar.
- **Down-bar**: a bar whose closing price is below the closing price of the previous bar.
- **Bar range:** the distance between the minimum and maximum prices of the bar. If the range is wide, the distance between the two levels will be large, and if the range is narrow, the opposite will be true.

These concepts, which may seem trivial, are extremely important in price analysis.

Taking this into account, if we now add volume analysis, we have two bars that are very characteristic in the market and that give many clues about the professional's strategy for the future:

- **No Demand:** this is a narrow-range up-bar, whose volume is lower than the volumes of the two previous bars.
- **No Supply:** this is a narrow-range down-bar, whose volume is lower than the volumes of the two previous bars.

Contrary to all rational thinking, all strength bars are down-bars, except for one, which we will see later.

Therefore, it is commonly said that strength in the market manifests itself in bearish bars and weakness in bullish bars.

Let us now look at all the strength bars that exist in the market.

2.1.1 BOTTOM REVERSAL

It occurs in market floors following a downward trend. If, when the time comes, we have a down bar and the next bar is an up bar whose range is equal to or greater than that of the previous bar, we will have a bottom reversal.

The strength lies in the fact that demand has entered the market in the bearish bar and has managed to overcome supply, for the moment, in the bullish bar (a consequence of the previous bar).

2.1.2 STOPPING VOLUME

Mid-to-wide range down bar with a close in the middle or upper part of the bar. The volume should also be relatively high.

The strength lies in the fact that demand entered at the bar's lows and achieved a close in the middle or upper part of the bar.

2.1.3 TEST

Narrow-range down bar with closure in the middle or upper part of the bar. The body of the test should not stray far from the closure of the previous bar.

The less volume it has, the stronger it is (genuine test).

2.1.4 ABSORPTION VOLUME

It is the only strength bar that is an up-bar. It is usually preceded by a structure where support and resistance levels are well marked.

The bar in question must be a wide-range, high-volume up-bar.

It is important to note that there must be a prior (re)accumulation structure, otherwise it could be considered a bullish false breakout if it is reversed.

2.1.5 BAG HOLDING

It is the strongest bar on the market. It is the only strength bar capable of changing the course of a downtrend, simply by its mere presence.

We could say that it is 'the mother of all strength bars'.

For it to occur, five requirements must be met:

- Previous downtrend.
- Down bar.
- Narrow range.
- In a new zone (there is no support on the left).
- Climatic volume.

2.1.6 SELLING CLIMAX

Down-bar preceded by a sharp downward impulse, where there is no subsequent result in the form of lower prices.

This is usually the first sign of strength in (re)accumulation structures, where market panic is evident.

2.1.7 SHAKEOUT

It can occur in an uptrend or in a (re)accumulation structure to the right of it.

It is, therefore, a down-bar that extends support lines, where strength has previously been seen.

It could also be said that it is a deliberate downward action by the market maker to encourage shorts (those betting on declines) and sweep out longs (those betting on rises).

2.1.8 NO SUPPLY / TEST IN A RISING MARKET

Down bar with lower volume than the previous two bars in an upward trend.

2.1.9 SUMMARY

In this way, we have already categorised the eight strength bars that exist in the market.

As we have seen, these eight strength bars are very different from each other. They all have their own particularities and must be added to our particular alphabet, which until now only had two letters: price and volume.

Table 1 provides a summary of these bars, based on the type of bar, its range, the type of impulse they are experiencing, and their volume.

Table 1: The eight strength bars

Strength bar	Type	Range	Previous trend	Volume
Bottom Reversal	Up-Down bars	Medium-wide	Downtrend	Medium
Stopping Volume	Down-bar	Medium-wide	Downtrend	Medium-high
Test	Down-bar	Narrow	Downtrend	Low
Absorption Volume	Up-bar	Wide	Range	High
Bag Holding	Down-bar	Narrow	Downtrend	High
Selling Climax	Down-bar	Medium-wide	Downtrend	High
Shakeout	Down-bar	Medium-wide	Range or uptrend	High
No supply / Test in a Rising Market	Down-bar	Narrow	Uptrend	Low

2.1.10 PRACTICAL EXAMPLES

Let's move on to the practical side, which is much more entertaining than the theory.

Next, we will show a series of enlarged charts, where we can detect the strength bars that have appeared throughout the chart.

Chart 5: Strenath bars (Robinhood)

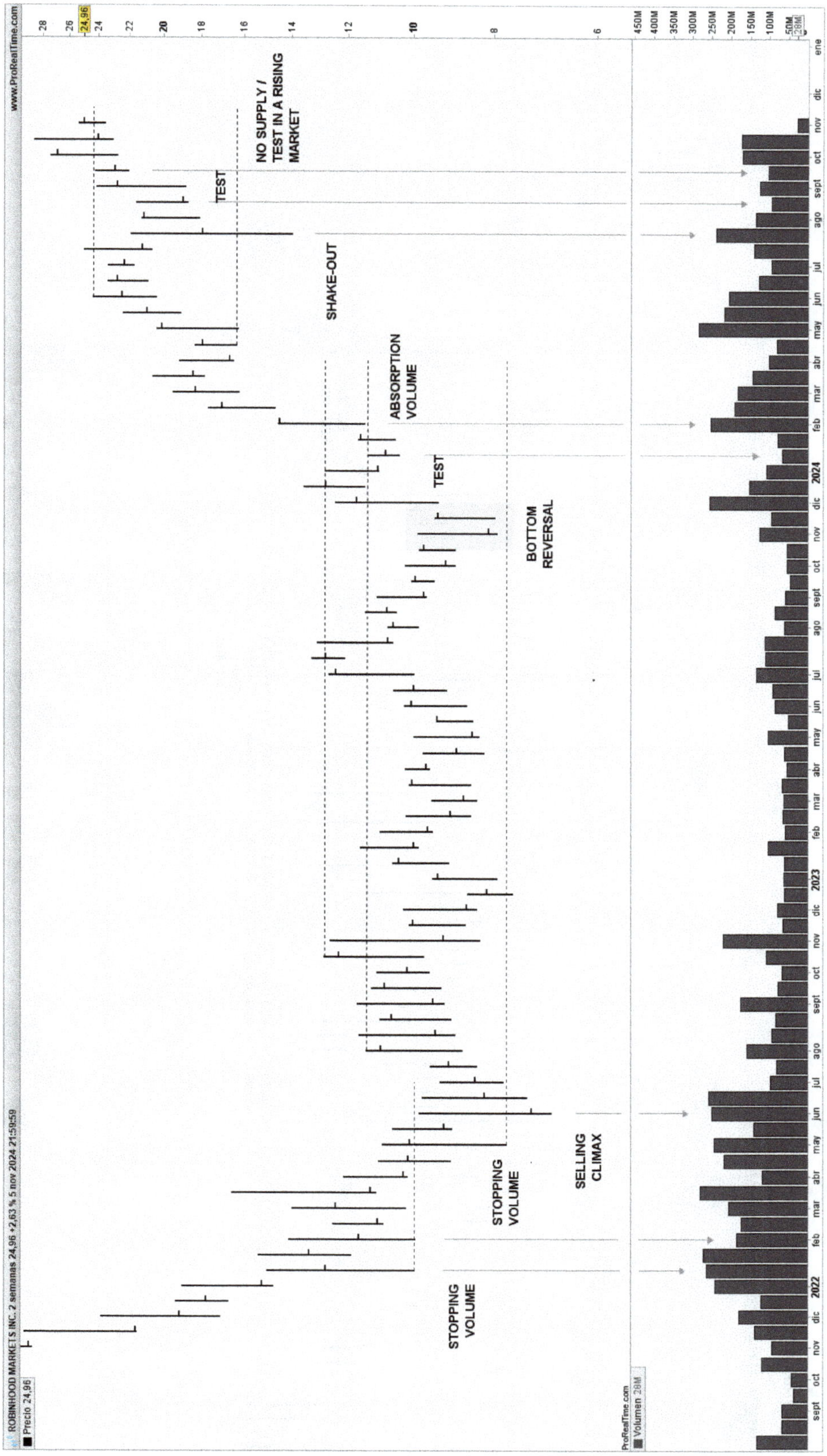

Chart 6: Strength bars (Monster Beverage)

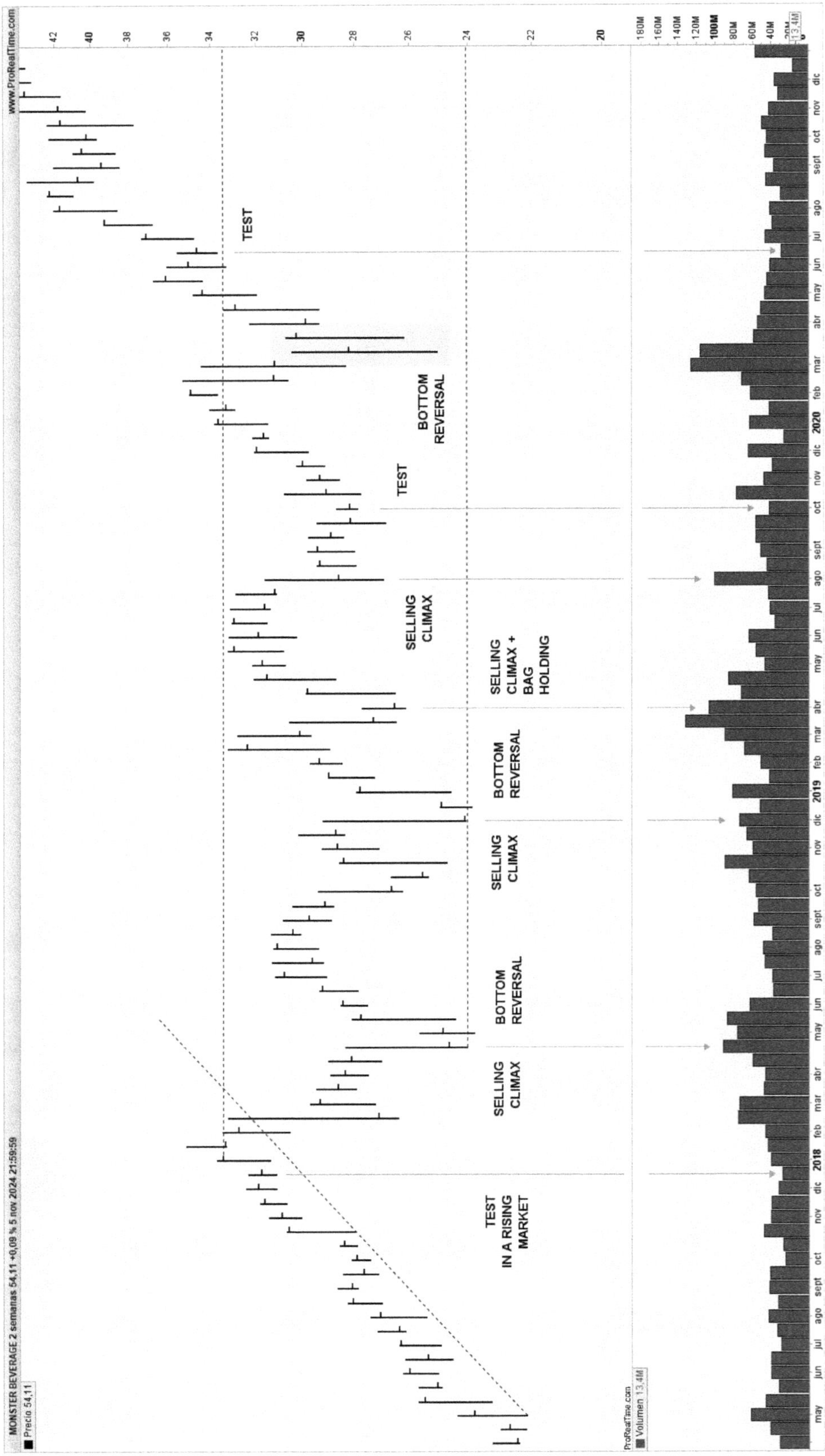

2.2 THE EIGTH WEAKNESS BARS

Once we have looked at the eight bars of strength, it is time to turn our attention to the eight bars of weakness.

As we know, the market is based on impulses and corrections, and these bars of weakness are due to the presence of supply in the asset. Therefore, all of them will be up-bars, except for one, which we will look at later.

2.2.1 EORM (END OF A RISING MARKET)

The 'End of a Rising Market' is the opposite bar to the 'bag holding' we saw previously. Therefore, it is the weakest bar in the market.

If we are facing an upward trend and suddenly see this bar on the chart, you should not ignore it.

It must meet the following five requirements:

- Previous uptrend.
- Up-bar.
- Narrow range.
- New zone (no resistance on the left).
- Climatic volume.

2.2.2 NO DEMAND AT MARKET TOP

It is an up-bar, narrow in range, smaller in volume than the previous two bars and located at market tops, indicating that professionals are not interested in seeing higher prices

2.2.3 NO RESULT FROM EFFORT

When an effort is made and there is no result, it could be said that the action taken has not been effective. In the market, this would translate into a mid-range up-bar with medium-high volume that cannot overcome resistance.

They usually occur at the top of (re)distribution structures.

2.2.4 UPTHRUST

It is a deliberate action by the market maker to encourage longs and sweep out shorts. It can occur in downtrends or to the right of a distribution structure (genuine upthrust).

Therefore, it is a medium-to-wide range up-bar, closing far from the highs and with climatic volume.

2.2.5 NO DEMAND IN A DOWNTREND

These types of bars are usually seen at the top of bearish channels or at the top of trading ranges.

It is a narrow-range up-bar with lower volume than the previous two bars.

It indicates that there is no professional interest in breaking resistance and that a bearish continuation is more than likely.

2.2.6 WIDESPREAD DOWN-BAR THROUGH PREVIOUS SUPPORT

It is the only down bar that shows weakness.

It usually occurs in (re)distribution structures or bullish channels. The price comes from the top, determined to break the support line. Therefore, it is a wide range down bar, closing near the lows and with climatic volume, which breaks a support line.

It is important to note that there must be a prior (re)distribution structure or bullish channel, otherwise it could be considered a bearish false breakout if it is reversed.

2.2.7 BUYING CLIMAX

Up-bar preceded by a sharp upward impulse, where there is no subsequent result in the form of higher prices.

It produces a change in behaviour and slows down the upward movement, indicating weakness in the price. The higher the volume, the greater the weakness.

2.2.8 TOP REVERSAL

It is an upthrust in two bars. It is a combination of an up-bar and a down-bar that occur at market ceilings after a substantial previous upward trend.

Weakness appears in the up-bar, and the down-bar is its consequence.

2.2.9 SUMMARY

In this way, we have categorised the eight bars of weakness that exist in the market.

Table 2 shows a summary of these, based on the type of bar, its range, the type of impulses in which they are found, and their volume.

Table 2: The eighth weakness bars

Weakness bar	Type	Range	Previous trend	Volume
EORM	Up-bar	Narrow	Uptrend	High
No Demand at Market Top	Up-bar	Narrow	Range - Uptrend	Low
No Result from Effort	Up-bar	Medium	Uptrend	High
Upthrust	Up-bar	Medium - Wide	Range - Uptrend	Medium-High
No Demand in a Downtrend	Up-bar	Narrow	Downtrend	Low
Widespread Down-Bar	Down-bar	Wide	Range - Uptrend	High
Buying Climax	Up-bar	Medium - Wide	Uptrend	High
Top Reversal	Up-Down bars	Medium	Range - Uptrend	Medium

2.2.10 PRACTICAL EXAMPLES

Now that we have seen the weakness bars, let's look at them graphically in real market cases.

First of all, you will have noticed that many of these bars, both weakness and strength bars, are similar to each other.

It is worth noting this, because it is a very interesting concept.

All bars have a unique and unmistakable character within the market. However, it is not enough to evaluate the strength or weakness of a bar on its own (even in 'bag holding' or EORM), but rather to evaluate the complete picture with the rest of the bars surrounding it.

So, if we see a potentially strong bar in a sea of bearish bars, we must quarantine the bullish reversal scenario.

There is a saying in the world of VSA that it is not very normal to see a polar bear in the desert. This metaphor is a great way to understand what I am trying to convey.

The bars, on their own, offer certain information. However, it is when taken that the signals left by the professional become clearer and more detectable.

I hope this message is clear, as it can be confusing the first few times we look at a chart with only price and volume information.

Moving on to the development of the concepts of weakness bars, some of them can be seen in the following charts.

All of them, taken as a whole, have caused the price to shift from a previous uptrend to a downtrend, which is why they are considered weakness bars.

Chart 7: Weakness bars (Taiwan Semiconductor)

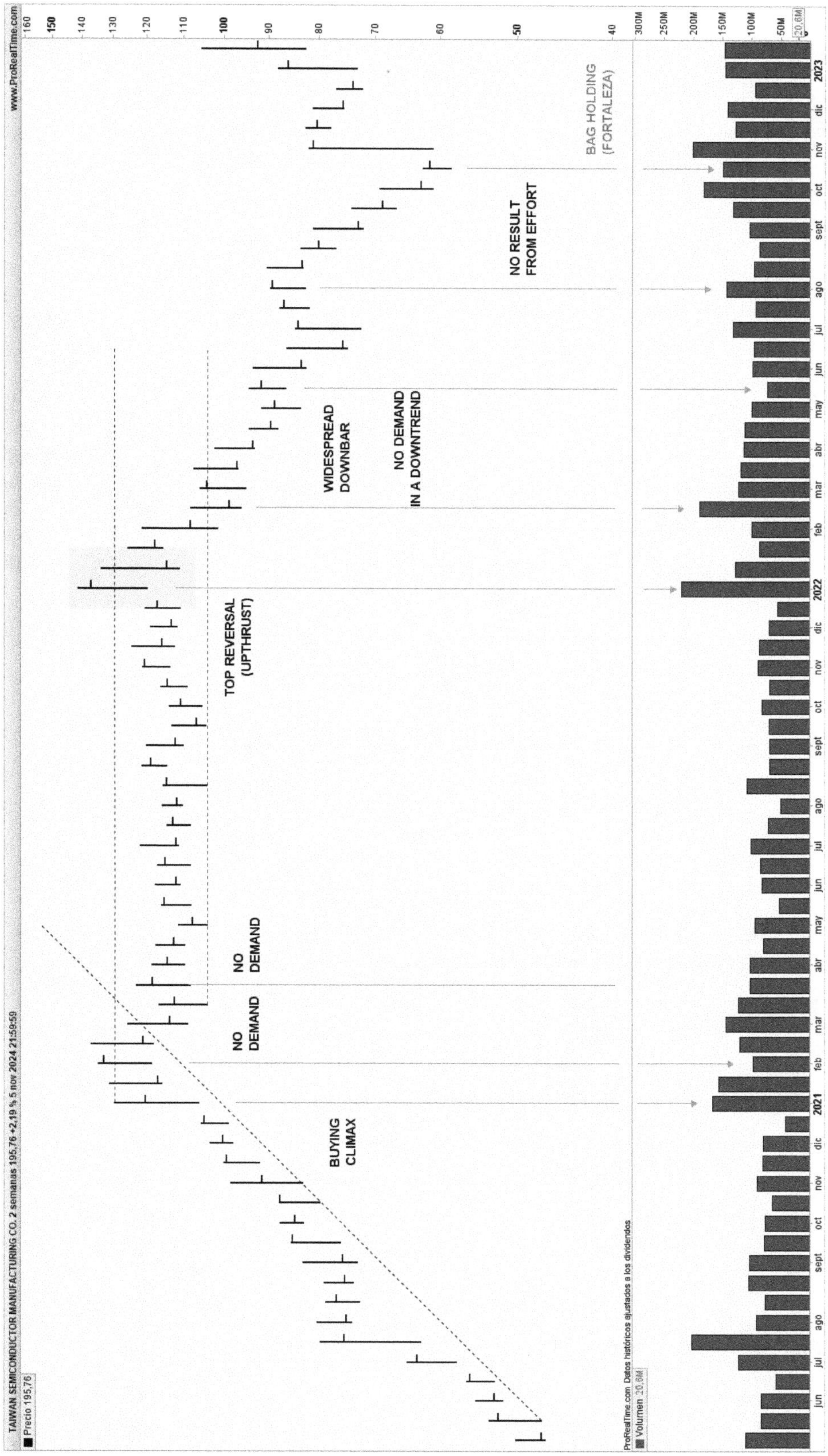

Chart 8: Weakness bars (Sea Limited)

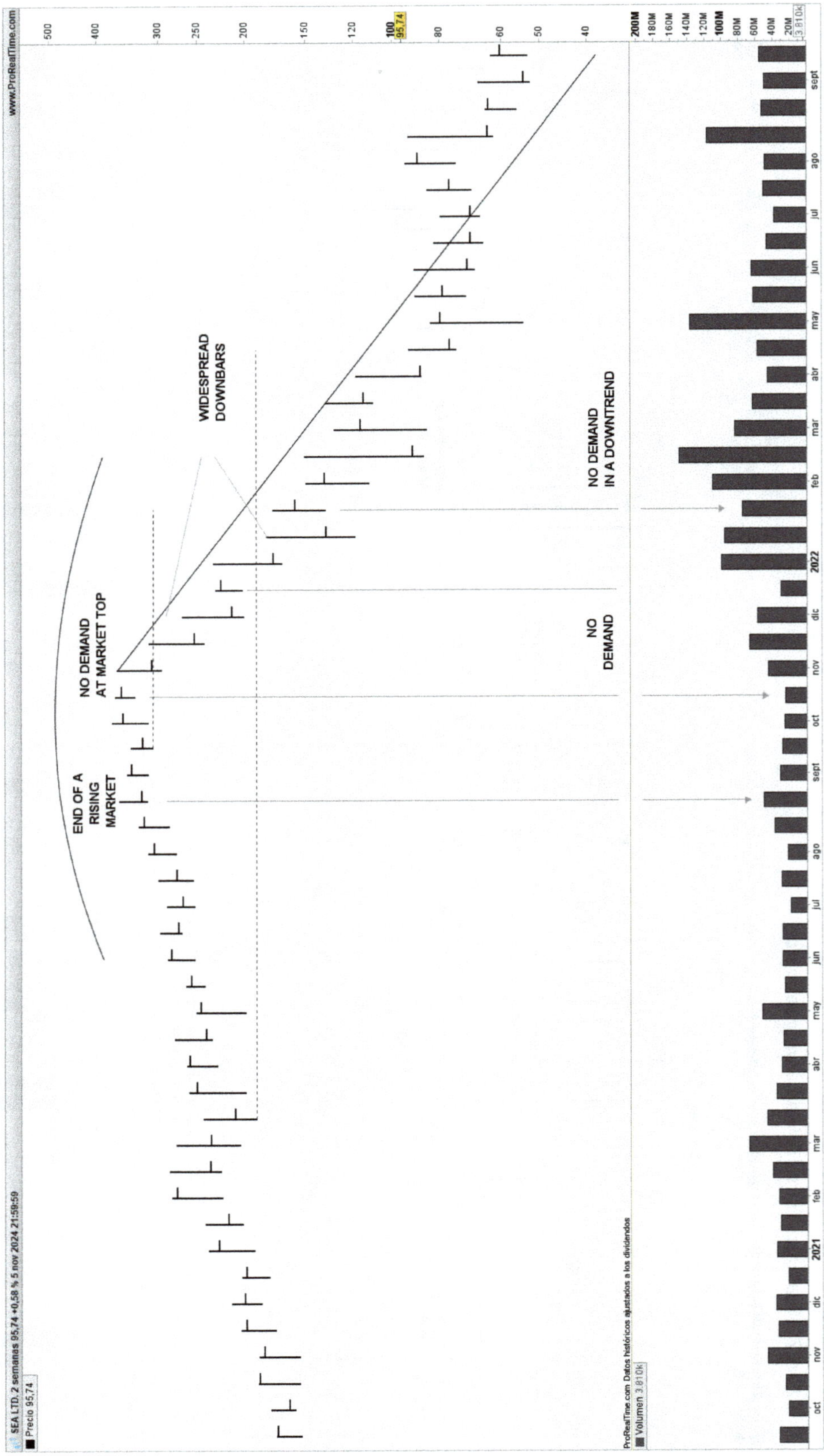

2.3 ACCUMULATION AND DISTRIBUTION PROCCESSES

Now that we know how to identify the types of bars that appear in the markets, it is time to look at the bigger picture.

A single bar on its own provides us with little valuable information to determine what the next price movement will be, as we have seen above. However, when viewed together with the rest of the bars, it gives us a complete picture of the current market situation and the possible intentions of the big players for the future.

Perhaps I am overemphasising this, but it is important that you internalise it as soon as possible.

When we analyse a chart, we have two distinct sides: the left side, where all the bars appear with their respective volumes; and the right side, which is blank. That is why it is vital to understand what is happening on the left side in order to make a hypothesis, based on the VSA methodology, of what the price may do on the blank side.

As we have no idea what the price will do in the future, we rely on this methodology to increase our chances of success. It is not an exact, mathematical science, but rather a methodology based on probabilities.

As we have seen above, prices move most of the time within trading ranges. These ranges, which are nothing more than support and resistance levels where the price moves from one side to the other without breaking either of them, are the cause of the subsequent price movement.

Once the range is broken on the upside or downside, an uptrend or downtrend begins that will have a run proportional to the cause.

Depending on the subsequent price movement, there may be accumulation, re-accumulation, distribution or re-distribution ranges, as can be seen in the next Chart 9.

Chart 9: Accumulation and distribution structures

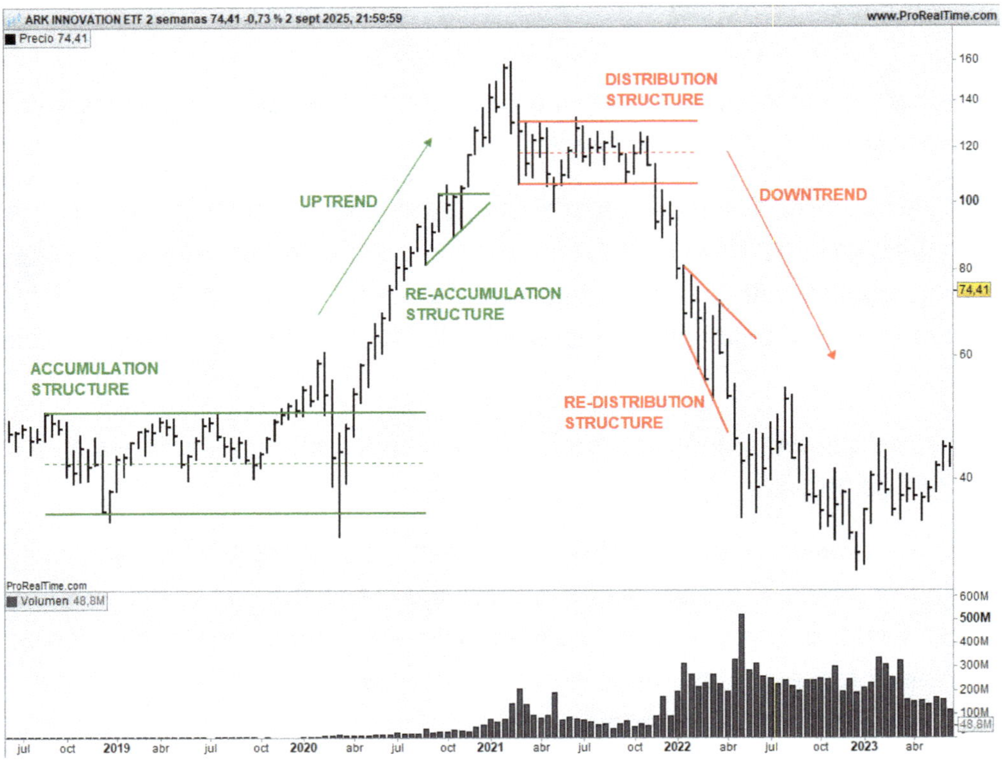

In a nutshell.

After a period of accumulation, an upward trend begins, which then pauses in its movement. A trading range occurs, and the price rises again, confirming the re-accumulation range. When the time comes, after a sharp upward movement, the price stops and moves sideways, forming another trading range. The subsequent movement is downward, confirming the distribution range. The price falls and slows down again, forming another range. After breaking out of it downward, it is confirmed that the range was one of redistribution. It will then fall again until it slows down and an accumulation range emerges (if it does so and the value does not go to zero).

And so on and so forth.

See how easy it is? Come on, let's close the book and go down to the pub for a few beers to celebrate that we now know everything about the market and that it's all that simple.

I'm sorry to say that I wish the real market were that easy. This is just a realistic representation of what accumulation and distribution structures are and their consequences. Often, the market is not that straightforward.

The bars widen the trading ranges and make it difficult to identify all the events. Only with experience and after looking at hundreds and hundreds of charts is the eye able to detect the trading ranges, so be patient and work hard.

Now let's say that the price is forming a trading range. We have identified it with the previous trend well defined. However, we do not know whether the trading range will be one of accumulation or distribution.

Making that distinction is not so easy. We must see where the highest volumes occur, determine whether the bars are strong or weak, and look at the picture.

To help us analyse each process, Wyckoff provided a series of concepts that we will look at below.

2.3.1 ACCUMULATION PROCESSES

Accumulation processes occur in markets with a previous downward trend. At a certain point, the price breaks the downward trend line, stops, and begins a trading range. In upward trends, re-accumulation processes occur.

Throughout this process, strong hands, for whatever reason, begin to accumulate shares or contracts of the asset, buying them from weak hands, who sell quickly in the face of the sharp falls that have occurred in the market.

This transfer of shares or contracts continues until a new imbalance is reached, where there are no more sales to be made and no more contracts to be bought. In other words, supply has lost control in favour of demand: supply has been absorbed by demand. At that point, once it has been verified that there is no supply in the market, demand has all the ingredients to rise without resistance.

That is one of the maxims of all this. The price follows the line of least resistance. At first, the line of least resistance was downward movements. Then, when the time comes, the forces balance out and demand gradually takes control of the situation, until supply disappears. At that point, the line of least resistance is on the upside, so the price has no choice but to start its upward trend, always proportional to the cause.

Wyckoff discretised the accumulation range as can be seen in Chart 10.

Chart 10: Wyckoff accumulation scheme

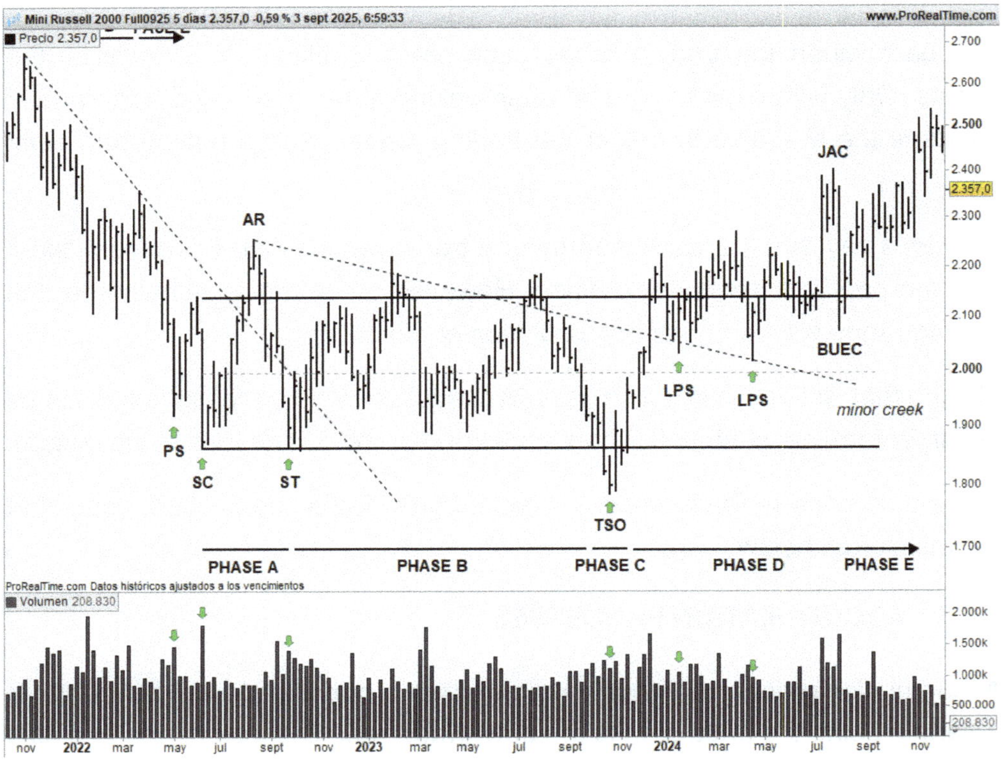

First of all, I have decided that all the examples we see in the diagrams will also be real market cases. There are numerous Wyckoff accumulation schemes on the Internet that you can consult whenever you want. However, you have to train your eye to see real cases of structures, in this case, accumulation.

In it, you can see five phases, which we will analyse later, as well as all the events that occur in each of them (the alphabet soup we will see below).

2.3.2 DISTRIBUTION PROCESSES

Distribution processes are the opposite of accumulation processes. They start with a sharp upward trend, where demand is in control of the situation. When the time comes, the price breaks the upward trend line, stops and remains within a trading range. Redistribution processes occur in downward trends.

Within this range, a battle ensues between supply and demand, where strong hands begin to sell shares or contracts to weak hands, eager to see the price continue to rise.

However, once the strong hands have sold all their stock, supply has taken control of the situation and the price has no choice but to follow the line of least resistance, in this case, downwards.

Once again, Wyckoff discretised the distribution ranges as shown in Chart 11.

Chart 11: Wyckoff distribution scheme

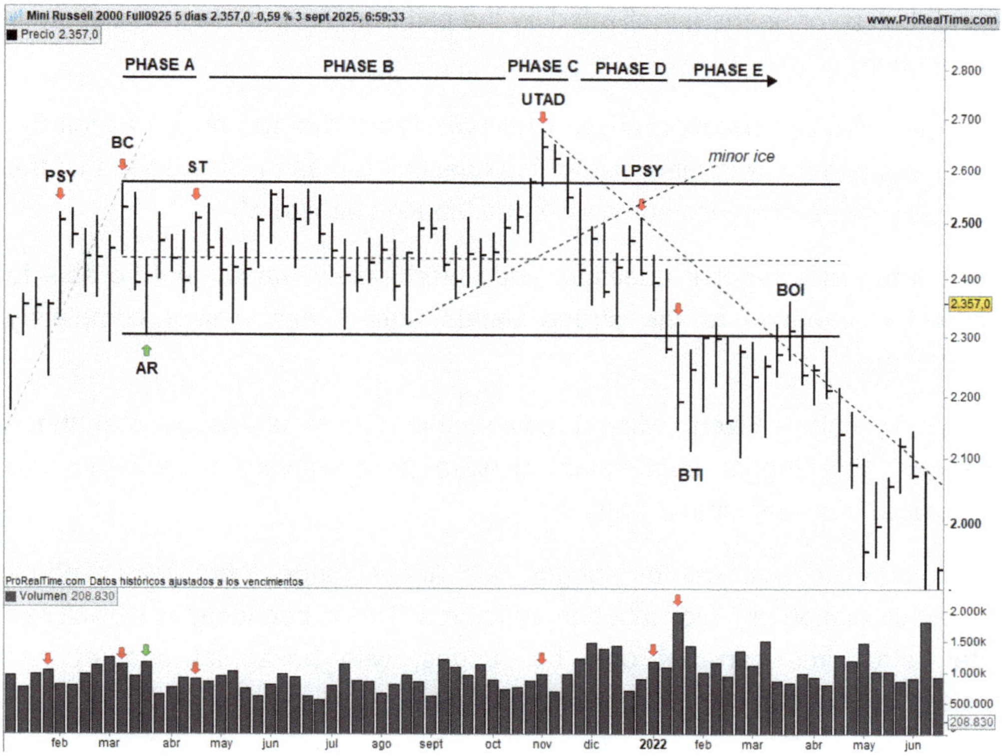

2.3.3 THE REAL TRADING

Needless to say, all these real cases you have just seen do not usually occur in such a neat and well-structured manner, despite being real cases.

On social media, whenever there is a mainstream value within a trading range, numerous diagrams appear that structure Wyckoff's accumulation and distribution processes. However, it is necessary to carry out a detailed analysis of all the bars that comprise it, rather than senselessly diagramming the structures.

In accumulation processes, we will see strength bars with volume peaks at the bottom of the range. Conversely, in distribution ranges, we will see weakness bars with volume peaks at the top.

Next, we will break down all the phases of Wyckoff's structures and analyse them separately to try to understand the entire structure.

2.4 WYCKOFF STRUCTURES IN DETAIL

Richard Wyckoff understood that the price of a stock market asset enters a trend (bullish or bearish) motivated by the exit from a range (accumulation or distribution).

However, the complication arises when we detect that the price has left the trend and entered a trading range. The question is clear: is the range that the price is moving in an accumulation or distribution structure?

That is the million-dollar question, and unfortunately, we will not be able to know the intention of the strong hands until it has almost completely developed.

What Wyckoff realized, without having the current charts, is that these "causes" that trigger subsequent upward or downward movements are structured in a very similar way.

From now on, we will no longer talk about ranges, but rather about (re)accumulation or (re)distribution structures. This is because, as we will see later, structures can not only be ranges, with horizontal support and resistance, but can also take different forms.

First, to simplify the process, we will take a horizontal structure like those we have seen in the accumulation and distribution processes and break it down into the different Wyckoff phases.

To do this, we will analyse both sides, the bullish side and the bearish side, so we will see the different phases with their respective nomenclatures for (re)accumulation and (re)distribution processes.

2.4.1 PHASE A

The first phase in a Wyckoff structure is Phase A.

This phase is characterized by a pause in price. The previous trend is pronounced, and there comes a point when the price exacerbates its movement. Immediately afterwards, there is a reaction in the opposite direction to the main trend, so that the price subsequently revisits the previous high/low.

We could say that the price has slowed down, has failed to continue with the previous trend, and has remained in a trading range.

2.4.1.1 Accumulation process

Let's assume that the trend is bearish and pronounced. Within an accumulation structure, we find the following events in Phase A:

- **Preliminary Support (PS):** this is preliminary demand, following a substantial downward price movement, where professionals are observing attractive buying zones. It is a first attempt by demand to stop the price, without success, which continues its downward trend.

  It is characterized by one or more down bars with relatively high volume and a brief subsequent upward reaction.

  Tom Williams, in his book Master the Markets, calls this bar Stopping Volume.

- **Selling Climax (SC):** this is the point of maximum panic in the bear market, where the news in the media is truly dramatic. It is characterized by a down bar preceded by a sharp downward impulse, where there is no subsequent result in the form of lower prices. Demand has entered to definitively stop the price, showing its strength in the final bar.

  The low or close of the SC will determine the minimum level of the trading range or accumulation structure.

- **Automatic Rally (AR):** after the SC, the price rises with relative strength, producing a short-range upward movement, motivated by the closing of short positions and professional buying. This is the effect of the Selling Climax. As the downtrend continues to prevail, the price is unable to continue its upward trajectory and slows down.
  The maximum level or close of this bar will define the upper end of the trading range.

- **Secondary Test (ST):** unable to continue its short-term upward trend, the price retests what lies behind it, which is the Selling Climax level. This retest should have a lower volume than the SC and preferably with narrow range bars.

  If the price can extend the low of the Selling Climax, it will indicate weakness in the subsequent structure. If, on the other hand, the ST does not approach the low of the SC, it will indicate strength in the subsequent structure.

2.4.1.2 Distribution process

Let's now look at the opposite case, where the price is in an uptrend and has already risen substantially. Within a distribution structure, we find the following events in Phase A:

- **Preliminary Supply (PSY):** this is the first sign that supply is entering the asset strongly. It is characterized by an up-bar with relatively high volume and a brief subsequent downward reaction. Supply is lurking.

- **Buying Climax (BC):** this is the bullish peak of the market. At this point, the news in the media is usually fantastic, with an aura that everything is in place and better than ever. This is the point where supply enters to slow down the upward trend. This produces an up-bar, after which there is no subsequent result in the form of higher prices. Supply is now very present in the market.

  The maximum level or close of the BC will mark the high point of the subsequent structure.

- **Automatic Rally (AR):** after the BC, there is a reaction in the price contrary to the main bullish trend, motivated by the closing of longs and the opening of shorts by professionals.

  The low of this bar will mark the low point of the subsequent structure.

- **Secondary Test (ST):** after the first bearish reaction, the price returns to its upward path and tests the close or highs of the BC, this time with less volume.

  If the price can exceed the BC high, it will indicate relative strength. If, on the other hand, the price is unable to approach the BC high, it will indicate weakness.

2.4.2 PHASE B

After Wyckoff Phase A comes Phase B. This is the area of struggle between supply and demand, the most time-consuming phase (in horizontal structures).

For a responsible trader, this is the zone where you should not trade. There are numerous deceptions on both sides, and the trend is sideways.

Trades should only be made if there are interesting configurations at the "riverbanks" (as David Weiss calls the extremes of the structures).

2.4.2.1 Accumulation and distribution process

Phase B is the trench phase. Bullish and bearish attacks, both for accumulation and distribution structures, are constant.

The main guideline of the previous impulse must be broken and supply absorbed (in accumulation structures), or demand eliminated (in accumulation structures), resulting in a decrease in volume throughout the price movement in the trading range.

During Phase B, the price moves from one side of the range to the other, and sometimes there are price expansions. These expansions are usually very short-lived, and the price returns to the trading range.

These expansions can be labelled as:

- **Upthrust Action (UA) or Upthrust in B (UB):** the price expands the upper part of the structure and then re-enters it.

- **Local Shake-Out (local SO):** the price expands the lower part of the structure and then re-enters it.

2.4.3 PHASE C

The third phase of Wyckoff is Phase C. After a stealthy battle between supply and demand in Phase B, there comes a point when one of the two sides finds an imbalance.

Translated into the world of boxing, imagine those endless fights in the ring between the Filipino and American boxers. Both are tired after a boring fight that has gone on for too many rounds. At one point, one of them throws a hook that misses its target and loses his balance. At that moment, the defender sees a unique opportunity to launch his attack with an advantage and rains down a flurry of punches that tip the scales in his favour.

Something like this but translated into the world of the stock market with supply and demand, could be metaphorically similar.

2.4.3.1 Accumulation process

This is the last test performed by demand within the structure.

Four types of events can be categorised in Phase C of an accumulation structure, all of which have a similar subsequent outcome for demand, which is none other than an upward breakout of the trading range.

Without this subsequent breakout, Phase C would not have had a place in the structure, and we would have had to wait longer to find a real imbalance between supply and demand.

Thus, in Phase C of an accumulation structure, we can find the following events:

- **Shake-Out No. 1 or Terminal Shake-Out:** there is a strong downward movement that breaks the base of the accumulation structure. As in the Selling Climax, the news is catastrophic and the price has already been consuming a lot of time and, therefore, pessimism in the value. However, the price recovers the base of the structure in the same bar or the next one, which indicates that everything that has happened was not on the supply side, but on the demand side.

- **Shake-Out No. 2:** in this case, the 'false break' movement of the base of the structure is not as abrupt as in the previous case. The price breaks down moderately, with relatively high volume, and the price hesitantly returns to recover the level of the base of the structure.

Numerous tests are carried out in the process to verify that supply has been absorbed by demand.

- **Shake-Out No. 3:** in this last case, during Phase B, supply has been absorbed, and the price reaches the base of the structure with little impulse, which breaks with little violence and returns to it.

  In this new 'false break', the candle ranges are narrow and with little volume, which does not indicate a true break intention.

- **Last Point of Support (LPS) or Spring Board:** the price is not even able to reach the bottom of the structure, because almost all the supply has been absorbed in the previous phase.

2.4.3.2 Distribution process

Seen from another angle, in distribution processes, the struggle between supply and demand in Phase B is also evident, with attacks on both the upper and lower parts of the structure. However, demand is becoming increasingly exhausted.

The final moment of this imbalance, as we mentioned earlier, occurs in Phase C, which in distribution processes has two possible events:

- **Upthrust after Distribution (UTAD):** this is analogous to the different shake-outs of an accumulation structure. After Phase B, the price decides to break the upper part of the structure, encouraging buyers to enter the market. However, the price quickly returns to the trading range.

  This is a bullish deception, as the subsequent movement causes the lower part of the structure to break.

- **Last Point of Supply (LPSY):** in this case, demand is completely exhausted, and the price does not have the strength to attempt to

approach the upper part of the structure, which indicates that there is no intention on the part of the strong hands to see higher prices.
The price slows down before reaching the top and begins its trajectory towards the bottom. It is very common to see No Demands on their particular downward path.

2.4.4 PHASE D

Wyckoff's Phase D (Mark down in a trading range) is characterised by being the continuation of the movement initiated in Phase C.

Returning to the boxer analogy, the defender dodged the attack and has now taken the initiative, cornering the opponent until he is pushed to the edge (of the trading range) and knocked out of the ring (outside the trading range).

2.4.4.1 Accumulation process

The price has suffered from the imbalance between supply and demand in Phase C, and demand now has a clear path to rise.

Within the trading range, there is usually a minor creek or internal downtrend line, which the price breaks as it moves towards the top of the structure.

On its upward path, as we have said, the price breaks through the top of the structure (the maximum or closing level of the Buying Climax that we have already seen) and begins its journey outside the trading range.

In Phase D of accumulation processes, two events occur:

- **Jump across the creek (JAC):** the creek or major creek is the top of the structure. Its similarity to a creek suggests that the price has been able to break through the top and is set to continue rising.
  This break can occur with a wide-range, high-volume up-bar candle (absorption volume) or with an upward gap.

- **Backup to the edge of creek (BUEC):** once the major creek has been broken, the price enters an upward trend. There are times when supply reappears after breaking through the upper part of the structure. At that point, demand must test whether there is supply in the market to follow the line of least resistance and retest the upper part of the already broken range.

This testing movement, which occurs with narrow-range, low-volume down bars (test), is called the BUEC of the structure.

2.4.4.2 Distribution process

In distribution processes, Phase D represents the victory of supply over demand. Demand has been exhausted and thrown off balance in Phases B and C, and now supply is in control of the situation.

Analogous to the creek in accumulation processes, in distribution processes there is the ice or major ice, which would be the lower part of the structure. Before this, there is usually an internal bullish guideline that is broken, called minor ice.

Thus, Phase D of distribution processes has the following two events:

- **Breaking the ice (BTI):** the opposite of JAC in accumulation processes. The price has already broken the minor ice and now breaks the lower part of the structure or the major ice.

- **Backing up to the ice (BOI):** the same as this event, opposite to BUEC. After breaking the major ice, demand makes an appearance and supply retests the broken level of the major ice. The price moves upwards with a withdrawal of volume (absence of demand) and falls again.

2.4.5 PHASE E

The final phase, Wyckoff's Phase E, is characterised by a clear trend following the price's exit from the trading range.

One of the two sides, supply or demand, has won the battle and is asserting its victory with broad and continuous movements.

2.4.5.1 Accumulation process

The price is already in an upward trend and only excessive supply can stop it. Throughout this process, there has been a shift in power from supply to demand, with the latter now in control of the situation.

Furthermore, the break in the structure in Phase D has already been confirmed and the price has a clear path to reach upward targets, following the line of least resistance.

During this upward journey, two events usually occur in Phase E:

- **Sign of Strength (SOS):** these are signs of strength once the major creek has been broken.

- **Last Point of Support (LPS):** these are simply the lows of the pullbacks and corrections of the upward impulses within the main upward trend.

2.4.5.2 Distribution process

The opposite of what we saw in the previous point. The price is in a downtrend and supply is in control of the situation.

In Phase E of a distribution process, the following events may occur:

- **Sign of Weakness (SOW):** the price develops a substantial downward trend, demonstrating weakness.

- **Last Point of Supply (LPSY):** the price, as in any trend, corrects the previous downward impulse, testing demand, which is not present in the value.

2.5 TYPES OF STRUCTURES

Until now, we have always talked about accumulation structures, distribution structures, trading ranges... However, we have not addressed the possible structures that appear in the market with a frequency that you cannot even imagine.

It does not matter what asset is being traded or what market it is in. It is something common to all liquid securities listed on the stock market that are governed by the law of supply and demand.

It also does not matter what time frame we are looking at. We have already mentioned that the market is fractal and that the price replicates the same structures over and over again, whether in five-minute or monthly charts.

Could we say that the strong hands are unoriginal? I would say no, that the market, in that sense, is very noble, but with many nuances.

It is true that on countless occasions they use different structures to mislead people. Although they may be unoriginal, they insist on distorting the patterns that appear in books and introducing dilations and imperfections.

In this section, we will detail the most common structures that can be found in the market. They are the most common and it is vital to identify them in order to detect where we are in the market.

This chapter will be very visual, with real examples. Schematic examples can be found on the internet in the blink of an eye and are useful for structuring ideas, but not for operating in the real market.

You must practise and look at real cases, because each asset tends to behave differently from another. Each one tends to repeat structures that may not be seen in others and vice versa. That is why it is key to train your eye.

2.5.1 HORIZONTAL STRUCTURES

These structures are classic. What we have seen so far could be perfectly applied to what we have called the trading range, in this case horizontal.

They are characterised by having the upper and lower levels of the structure horizontal and parallel to the time axis on the x-axis.

They are the easiest to detect and the most common in the markets. They repeat themselves over and over again, and if we can detect which phase we are in, we will have a significant advantage.

Let's look at a couple of examples of horizontal structures, both accumulation and distribution, to put into practice everything we have learned so far.

On the next page, we see the Robinhood chart, a stock listed on the NASDAQ. In it, you can see a perfect and clear horizontal accumulation structure.

Not all market structures are the same. In this case, we have a redistribution structure before the SC that momentarily slows the decline. That entire structure could be considered a PS.

Later, after performing the SC and AR, the ST acts as bag holding and breaks the SC lows, denoting apparent weakness. However, it was all a deception, as bars later the price remains in the trading range, forming a Wyckoff horizontal structure.

The supply is absorbed throughout the structure and dilations occur at the top in the form of UA.

Phase C occurs with an LPS, which causes the price to change character and break the top of the structure.

Subsequently, supply re-enters the stock and slows its advance, which again forms another horizontal re-accumulation substructure, confirmed after a large TSO in its Phase C. All of this is structured within a bullish channel.

Chart 12: Horizontal structure (Robinhood)

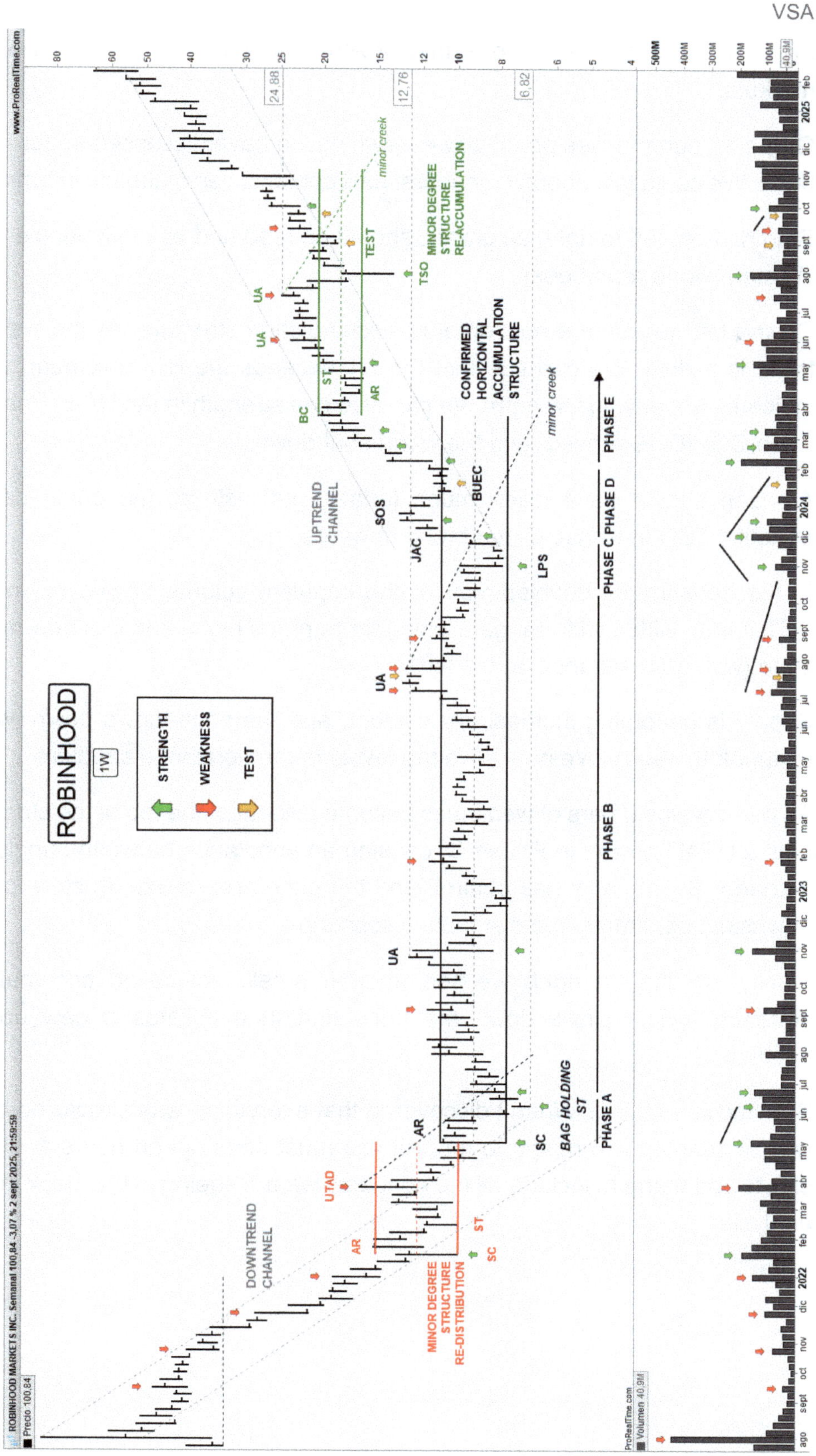

An even more curious case is that of Amazon, which is also listed on US markets.

Graph 13 summarises practically everything we have discussed so far in this book. We could talk about it for hours, as it contains very valuable information.

Starting from left to right, as graphs should be read and as most people in the Western world read books.

On the left, we have a horizontal re-accumulation structure, as the previous trend is bullish. We can see that the ST exceeds the BC maximum, which indicates underlying strength. We can also see strength in the UA in Phase B. Then COVID-19 arrived, and the world shut down.

Amazon should have fallen much further, but instead, the price made a beautiful TSO in Phase C and broke upwards.

In the subsequent development of the impulse, volume begins to enter in bullish bars with a wide range, closing far from the highs and in a new market zone (with no resistance on the left).

Supply is becoming increasingly evident, and the price slows down, with a textbook Phase A. We now have the levels of the horizontal structure.

As this develops, bars of weakness become evident at the top of the structure, until a UTAD occurs in Phase C, causing an imbalance between supply and demand. Supply now has control, and the price breaks the structure on the downside, confirming the distributive scenario.

Finally, on the far right, we see another small, unlabelled accumulation structure, which slows down the price and then initiates a new upward impulse.

Spectacular, isn't it? When I discovered that everything was structured in this way, it seemed like magic to me. All you must do is spend hours analysing charts and trying to include all the concepts we are seeing in this book in your analysis.

Chart 13: Horizontal structures (Amazon)

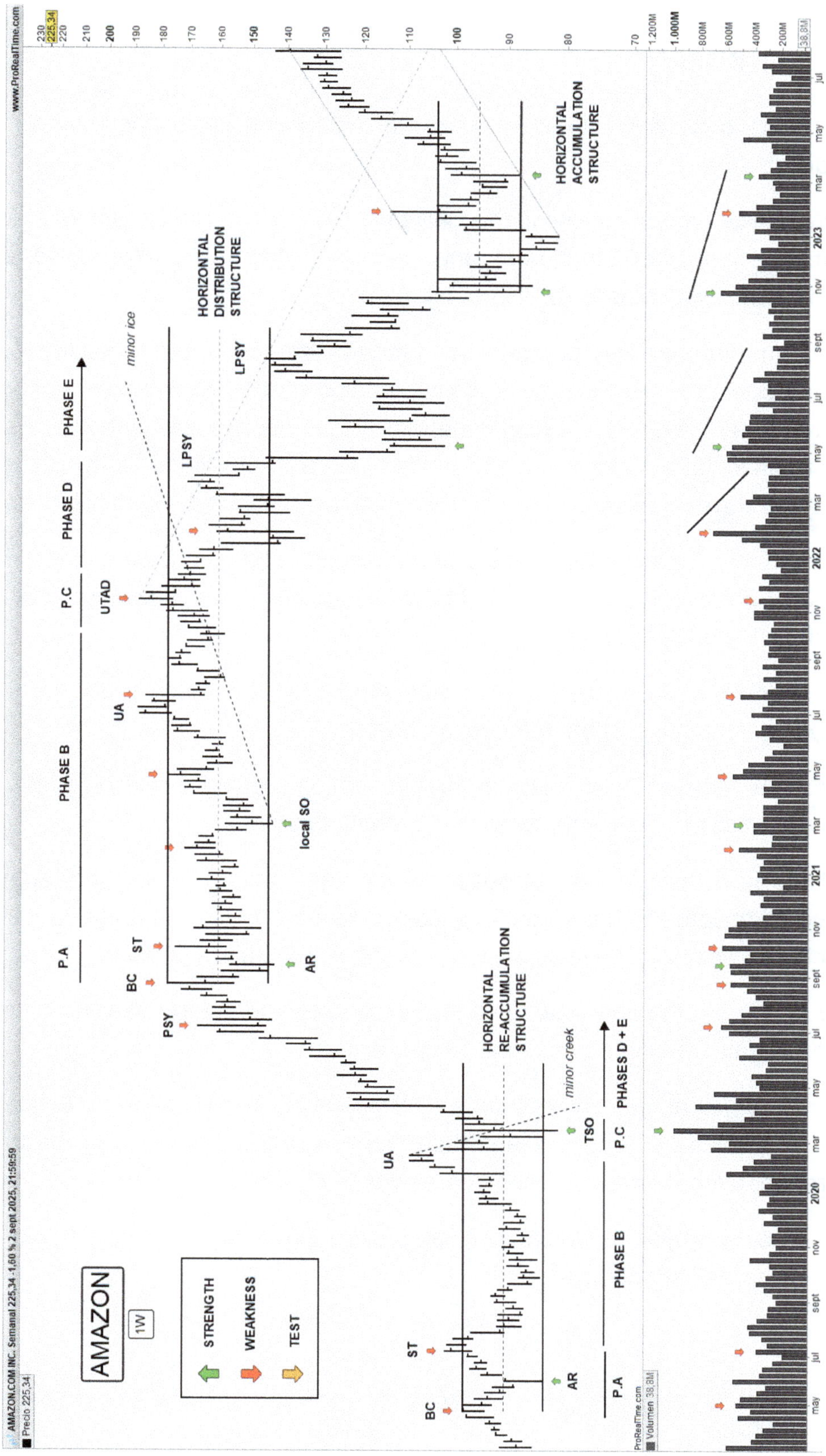

2.5.2 HORIZONTAL STRUCTURES WITH UPWARD OR DOWNWARD BIASES

We have already looked at horizontal structures, both accumulation and distribution.

Well, like everything else in this universe, there are certain nuances to add to these horizontal structures, and they are their twin sisters: horizontal structures with biases (bullish or bearish).

When a trend is very pronounced, it means that one of the two sides (supply and demand) has the situation well under control. If at any point during this trend there is a pause, i.e. the strength of the opposite side is tested, a series of horizontal structures usually appear that are not parallel to the x-axis but rather develop along a kind of bullish or bearish channel with a slight slope.

It can thus be said that if the horizontal structure has an upward bias, it has a slight positive slope, and if the horizontal structure has a downward bias, its slope is negative.

This may seem a little convoluted in words, but it is much easier to explain with examples, such as the one in Chart 14.

In it, we see an asset that, on the left side, is forming a horizontal structure with a bearish bias, structured in a bearish channel.

Note how the volume decreases as the value falls, showing that supply is being absorbed. There comes a point when the price has done its job and, after Phase C, it breaks upwards, starting a new bullish phase.

From there, the price rises and supply re-enters the stock, slowing down the price and creating a horizontal structure.

In fact, we can see bullish bars with climatic volume that denote weakness. A potential UTAD occurred, and the price has broken the base of the trading range, even with tests already underway.

It seems only a matter of time before the price resumes its decline, now outside the structure.

Chart 14: Bearish bias structure (Amark Precious Materials)

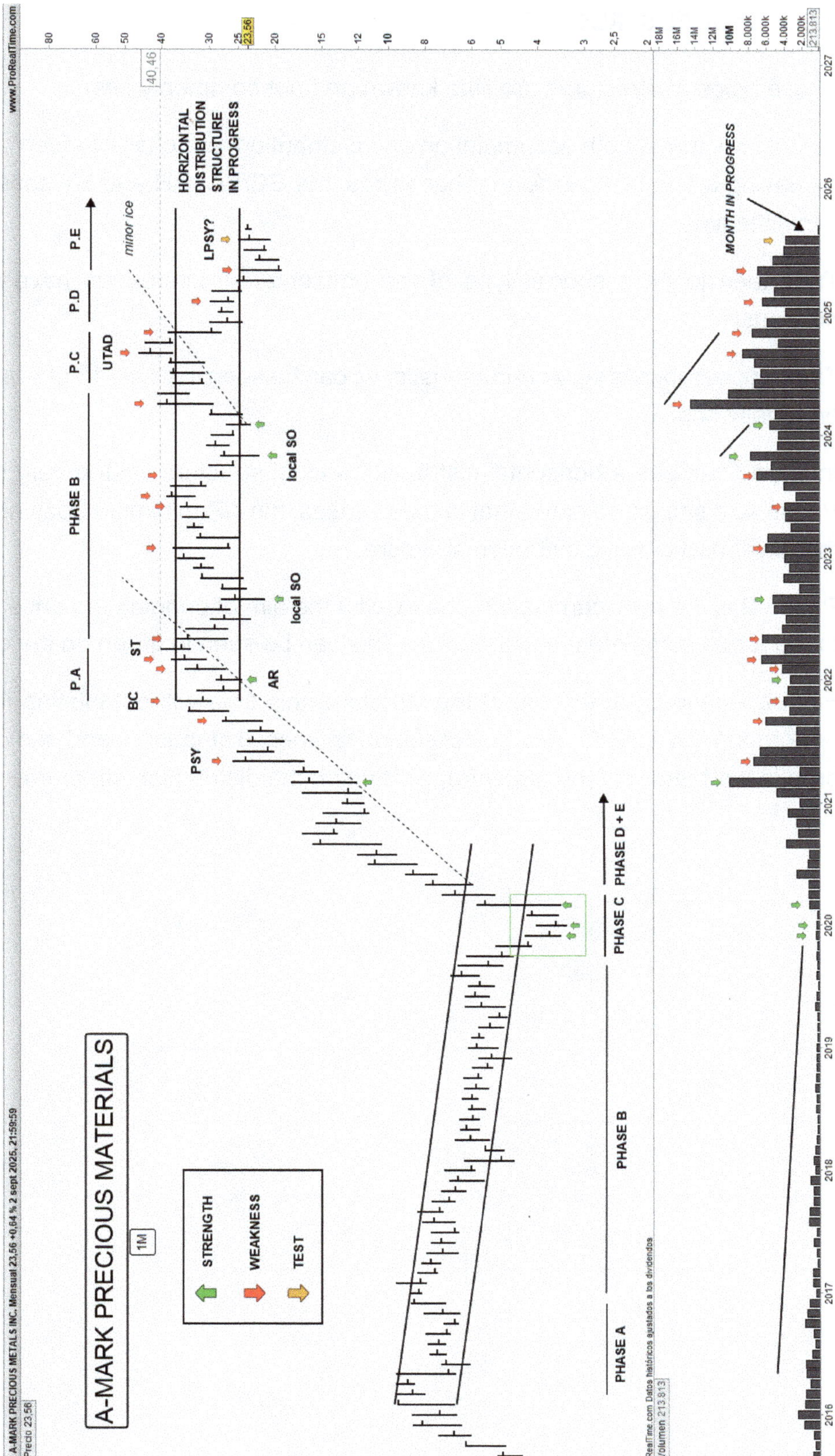

2.5.3 MODEL STRUCTURES

These types of structures are little known and not commonly seen.

Model structures, both accumulation and distribution, are characterised solely by having a short Phase A. In other words, the SC/BC, AR and ST consume very little time.

They tend to be a special type of the horizontal structures we have seen previously.

Their appearance is very characteristic, as can be seen in Chart 15 of Amazon on a daily basis.

In it, you can see a horizontal distribution model structure, with a very small Phase A. It should be noted that in these cases, the AR minimum does not set the lower part of the distribution structure.

Phase B is the re-accumulation phase, with the aim of bringing the price back to the top to complete the distribution. This can be seen in green on the chart.

Finally, Phase C, at the top of the structure, this time without dilating it and performing an LPSY. The professional finishes distributing and the price breaks the bottom of the structure, confirming the distribution structure.

Chart 15: Model structure (Amazon)

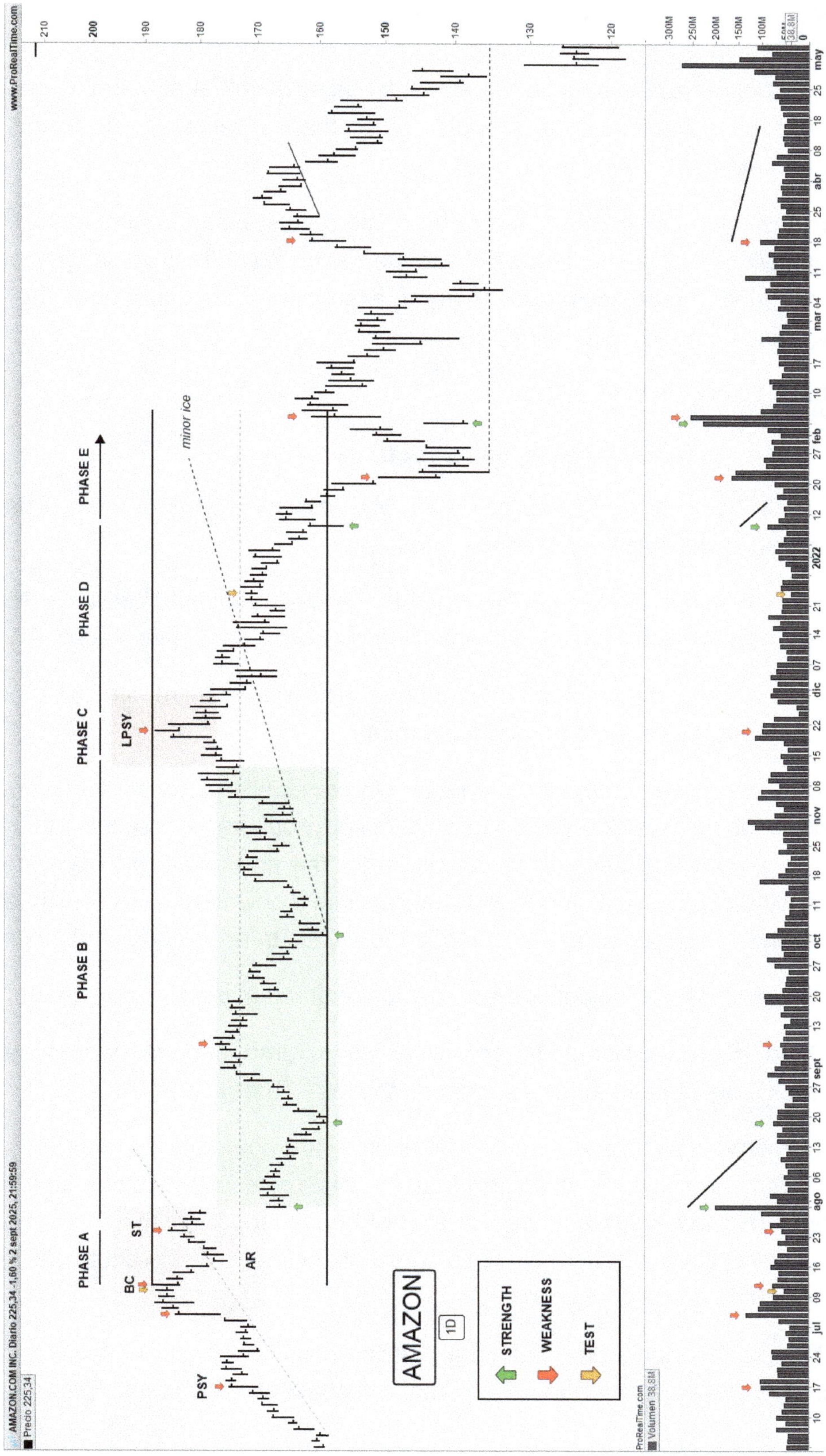

2.5.4 TRIANGULAR STRUCTURES

Leaving horizontal structures behind, let us now look at structures where the predominant shape is a triangle rather than a rectangle (reducing it to geometry).

In this type of structure, the price contracts or expands according to two guidelines that are not parallel. Thus, we can have contractive triangles, where the price compresses over time, or expansive triangles, where the price expands between two guidelines.

Let's look at them in detail.

2.5.4.1 Contractive triangular structures

These types of structures are relatively easy to detect. In them, Phase A usually takes little time, as does Phase B.

Everything moves faster in this type of movement than in Elliott Wave Theory, which we will see in the next chapter, where it develops in five stages, ABCDE.

In this case, there is a level around which the entire structure pivots, compressing the price around it over time.

Thus, we have contracting triangular structures with a horizontal pivot level, which usually break in the direction of the previous trend; triangular structures with an upward bias, which usually imply the end of the previous impulse (ending action); and triangular structures with a downward bias, which tend to resolve in the opposite direction of the previous trend (also ending action).

Let's look at a very useful example to understand this type of structure.

Chart 16: Banco Santander on a weekly timeframe (each bar represents one week). Do you see the sharp drop on the left? That is COVID-19.

The world was in panic mode at that time, and the declines were in double digits. There comes a point when the market enters a state of extreme volatility, with rises and falls in a very short period of time. A contracting triangle, terminal structure or ending action, whatever you want to call it, was beginning to form.

The price, in turn, experienced a drastic reduction in volume, indicating that supply was being absorbed. The subsequent movement was just as explosive: the vaccine against the virus was discovered. Could this have been predicted by looking at the chart alone? I'll leave that up to you.

Afterwards, the price made an upward move that ended with supply re-entering the stock. From there, a horizontal structure with a downward bias formed, structured in a downward channel.

It can be seen that, during the price's movement through this structure, the volume was drying up, indicating little interest on the part of professionals in seeing lower prices.

Upon reaching Phase C of the structure, the price broke upwards and began a new impulse.

Once again, supply entered the stock, and this time the price began to experience horizontal resistance and increasingly higher lows. This formed another re-accumulation structure in the form of a contracting triangle. It is characterised by increasingly higher lows, an effect of demand being very present in the stock and pushing the price upwards, compressing it against the horizontal resistance.

Once the supply has been absorbed, the price breaks upwards through the resistance or upper part of the structure and tests it, thus continuing its upward trajectory.

All this has happened in a single chart, three different types of structures with many substructures that we have not discussed and that are in the chart if we look closely.

That is why I say that it is vitally important that you put into practice everything we are seeing in the book, so that you get used to identifying all types of structures at a glance.

Chart 16: Contractive triangular structures (Banco Santander)

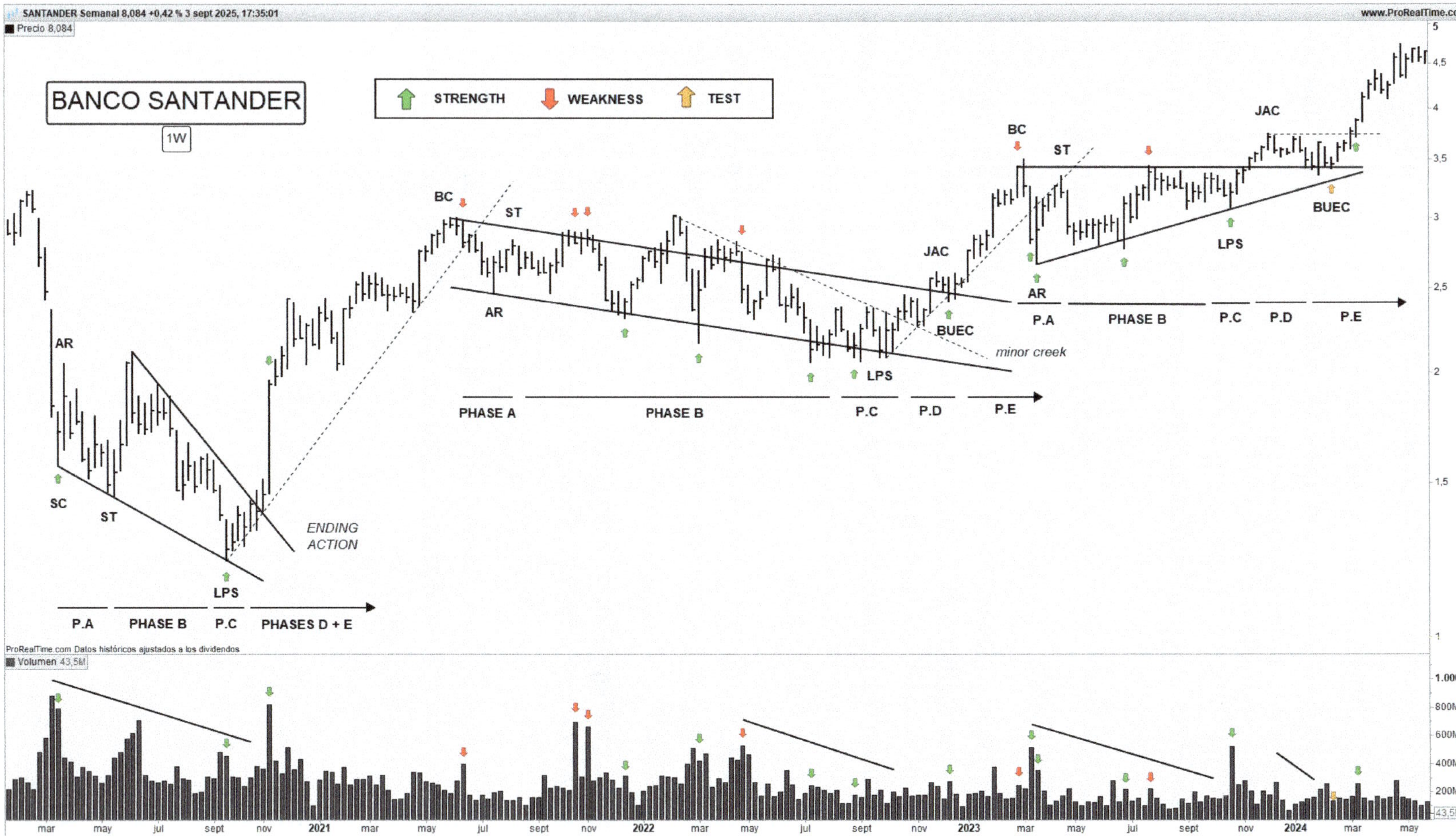

2.5.4.2 *Expansive triangular structures*

These types of structures are less common in markets and are most prevalent in previous uptrends.

We start with an upward impulse, and the price slows down. From there, it usually makes a movement that is stuck between two non-parallel guidelines that tend to expand over time.

These types of structures also tend to develop in five waves or internal movements, in the form of ABCDE.

Generally, their subsequent movement is in favour of the previous trend. They tend to test the investor's patience, as they usually take a long time to develop.

Let's look at a practical example of this.

Chart 17. Here is Bitcoin against the US dollar on a two-day chart (each bar represents two days).

From left to right, as always. Horizontal re-accumulation structure with a TSO in Phase C. This caused a flawless upward impulse.

Again, as with any finite impulse, supply appeared and stopped the price. So much so that it broke the upward trend line and the price began to expand between two non-parallel trend lines (expanding triangle).

You can see how the triangle was composed of five ABCDE waves, characteristic of this type of structure.

The price moved from one side of the triangle to the other, with decreasing volume (drying up of supply). When the time came, prompted by bearish news in the media, the price broke through the bottom of the structure and quickly recovered. This produced a TSO, and from then on, the price began to make higher highs and higher lows.

Then, the price broke upward after briefly testing the breakout. Textbook stuff.

Chart 17: Expansive triangular structures (Bitcoin / USD)

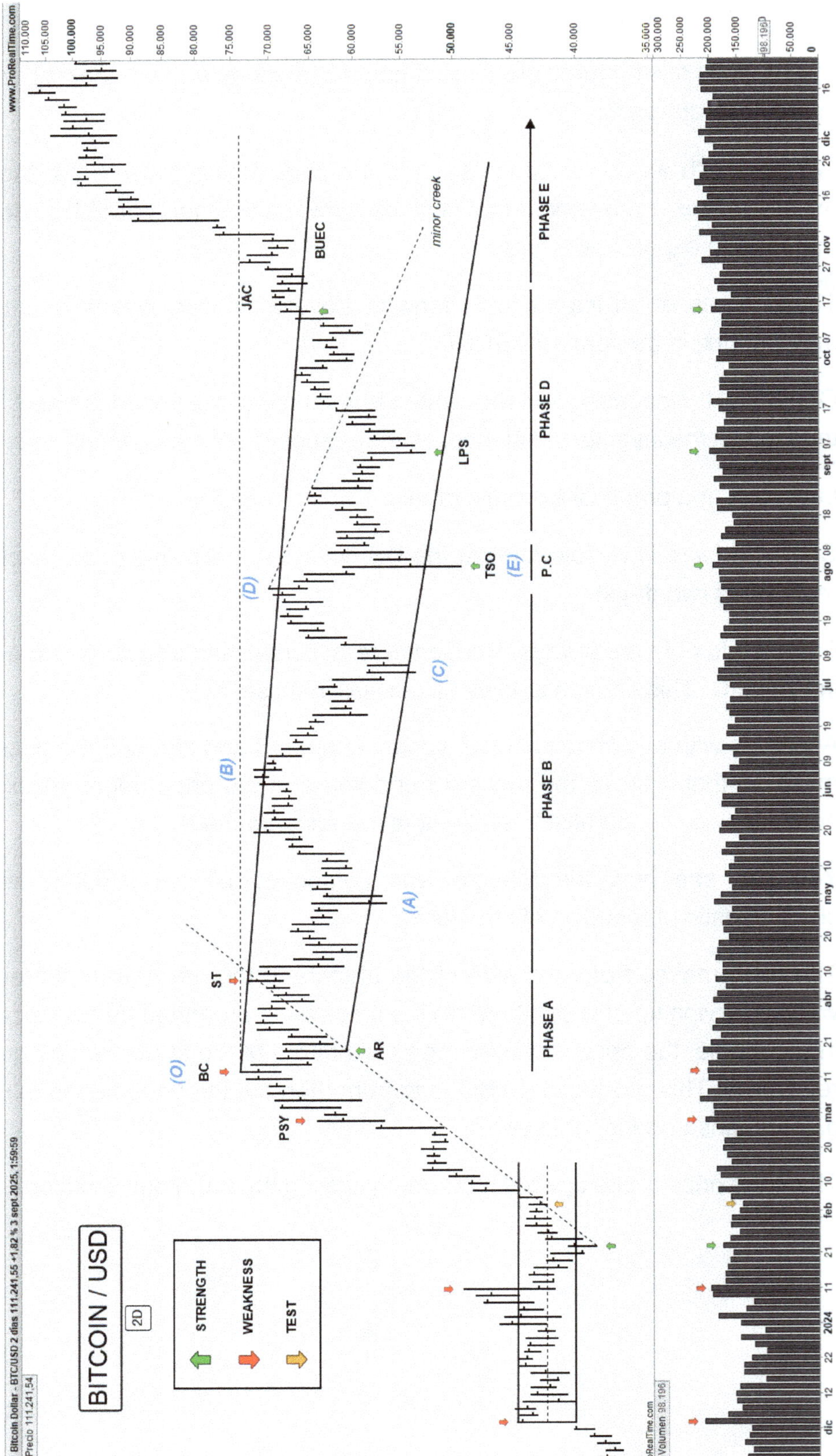

2.5.5 HEAD AND SHOULDERS STRUCTURES

The mother of all structures, as my mentor would say. And no wonder, because the impact that these types of structures have on price is enormous.

These are the head and shoulders (H&S) in distribution processes and the inverted head and shoulders (iH&S) in accumulation processes.

They are still horizontal structures (with or without bias), where in Phase B the price greatly expands the upper or lower part of the structure.

As always, it is best to look at graphic examples to see what we are talking about.

Let's look at a first example of H&S.

Chart 18. We return to the COVID-19 era and now analyse the Russell 2000, which brings together the 2,000 largest small and mid-cap companies in the United States.

The market was immersed in an impeccable uptrend. However, as in all distributive processes, bullish bars with climatic volumes and No Demand bars began to appear. So much so that the price broke the uptrend line and a trading range occurred.

In that structure, Phase B had a large expansion at the top, which quickly came to nothing. After a few bars, the price attempts to attack the top again, once more without success.

Note the drying up of volume each time the price attempted to attack the top. This is very characteristic of H&Ss. Volumes decrease as the left shoulder, head and right shoulder develop, showing the absence of demand.

Then COVID-19 arrives, and the price breaks the base of the structure with a gotcha bar (widespread down-bar through previous support) and produces large declines.

Could the sudden movement of such random news as COVID-19 have been predicted by analysing the chart alone?

I'll leave that question there again.

Chart 18: H&S Structure (Russell 2000)

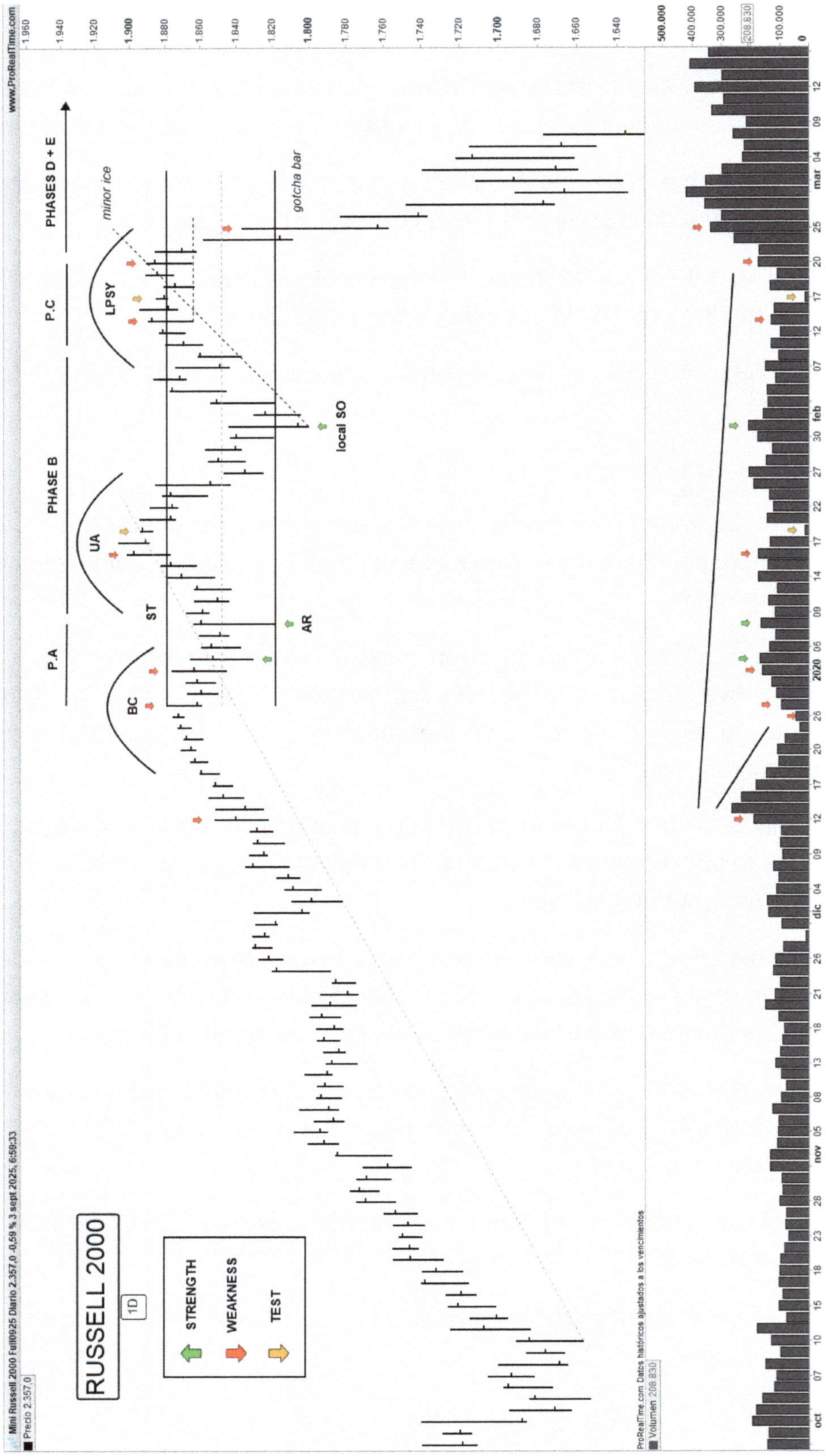

Let's now move on to a more advanced chart that previews concepts from Elliott Wave Theory, which will be explained in the next chapter.

In Chart 19, we have Coinbase. Many of you who trade in the crypto market are probably familiar with one of the world's most famous exchanges.

Its journey on the stock market has not been entirely smooth. Since it went public, there was a time when everyone wanted to have it in their portfolio, only to immediately revile it.

The price has not stopped falling since the IPO (Initial Public Offering). If you look closely, you will see that an expanding triangle formed a distribution structure with five segments: ABCDE.

Subsequently, the price plummeted, and another expanding triangle formed, causing the final drop in price.

However, there came a point when demand entered the scene and began to form a trading range.

In the middle of Phase B, a price expansion created the head of the future inverted H&S. In Phase C, the price could not even attack the bottom of the structure, leaving an LPS (Spring Board). Joining the two shoulders' highs and drawing the trend line gives us the inverse H&S neckline, which acted as a minor creek for the entire accumulation structure.

The price broke upwards and retested the neckline, which had already been broken. Interestingly, that BUEC of the structure formed a re-accumulation substructure (marked in blue), which dried up all the supply in the market.

The outcome was more than obvious. The price broke upwards strongly, leaving behind a perfect accumulation structure in the form of an inverted head and shoulders.

Chart 19: Inverted H&S structure (Coinbase)

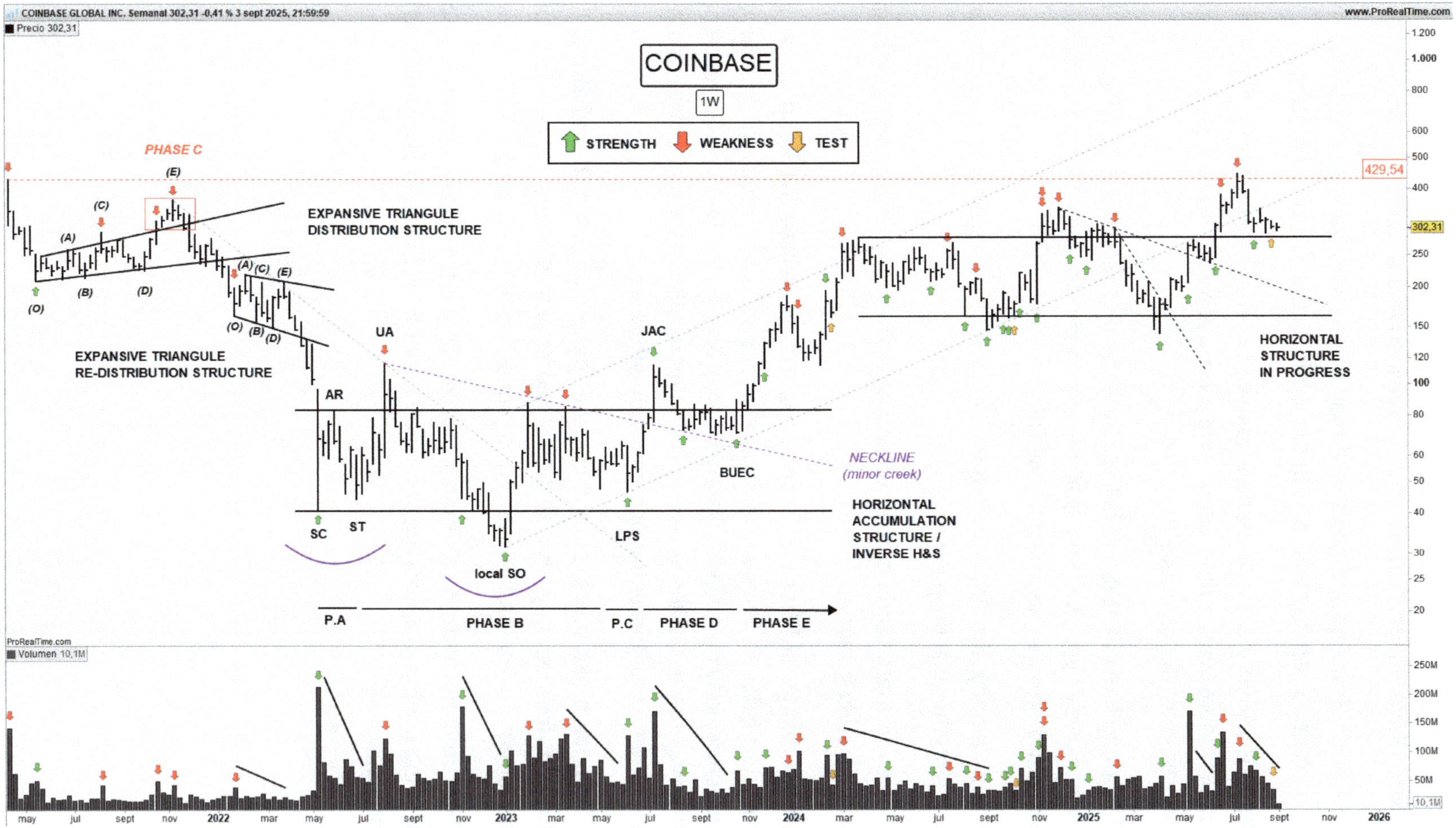

2.6 THE NINE TESTS OF WYCKOFF (STRENGTH)

As we have seen in previous chapters, Richard Wyckoff was ahead of his time. He created his own way of reading the market by analysing price and volume, something that was very complicated at the time, when modern stock market charts did not exist.

As part of his analysis of bars and volume, he created a kind of checklist that served to identify both market bottoms and tops.

This list consists of nine facts or events that must occur in the market for an uptrend or downtrend to form.

This is very useful for identifying entries and exits, the two operations that a trader must master, because that is what this business is all about: making money from the trades we make.

Well, according to Richard Wyckoff, for a market bottom to occur and the previous downtrend to reverse, the following questions must be answered in an accumulation structure.

The nine tests of Wyckoff (strength)

1. Has the price reached the bullish downside target (using a point and figure chart) or has the price previously made a substantial downward move?
2. Is there evidence that the price is being held back by demand? (Preliminary Support; Selling Climax; Automatic Rally; Secondary Test)
3. Is there bullish activity? That is, does volume expand when it rises and retreat when it falls?
4. Has the bearish trend been broken?
5. Are there higher lows?
6. Are there higher highs?
7. Does the asset have relative strength?
8. Has a base been formed?
9. Is the estimated upside potential greater than the downside potential?

If, when analysing a chart, you have been able to answer all the questions on the list favourably, then you are most likely looking at a market bottom.

The sharp downtrend has slowed, and the impulse has gradually shifted from the supply side to the demand side, until the latter has taken control and the price has reversed its upward trend.

Combining the above, it can be seen from the list that entries that are favourable for the trader on the long side are in Phases C, D and E. Therefore, long entries should be avoided during accumulation processes in Phases A and B.

2.7 THE NINE TESTS OF WYCKOFF (WEAKNESS)

Now let's look at the opposite scenario. We are coming off a very sharp uptrend and the first signs of weakness are appearing. Are we facing a market top?

In this case, Wyckoff also provides us with a list of nine events that you should identify to know if we are at a market top and how to profit from short positions.

The nine tests of Wyckoff (weakness)

1. Has the price reached the upside target (using a point and figure chart) or has the price previously made a substantial upward move?
2. Is there evidence that the price is being held back by supply? (Preliminary Supply; Buying Climax; Automatic Rally; Secondary Test)
3. Is there bearish activity? In other words, does volume expand when the price falls and retreat when it rises?
4. Has the upward trend been broken?
5. Are there lower lows?
6. Are there lower highs?
7. Does the asset have relative weakness?
8. Has a ceiling been formed?
9. Is the estimated downside potential greater than the upside potential?

Again, if we answer yes to all these questions, we are probably facing a market ceiling.

The uptrend has slowed over time until supply has taken control of the situation. At that point, a downtrend is very likely to begin.

Taking all this into account, once again, the best downward or short trades occur in Phases C, D and E of the distribution structure.

3. ELLIOT WAVE THEORY

Now that we have taken a detailed look at the entire universe of possibilities offered by Wyckoff's VSA, I have decided to include in this book a brief description of the world of Elliott Wave Theory.

If you are interested in delving deeper into the world of Elliott, I highly recommend reading the book 'Teoría y Práctica Moderna de las Ondas de Elliott' (Modern Theory and Practice of Elliott Waves) by Óscar G. Cagigas. For me, it is the bible of Elliott Waves, and you can find many practical examples that are then replicated, with their nuances.

That said, Elliott Wave Theory seeks to structure price trend movements. This is an important difference. It does not study the behaviour of trading ranges like Wyckoff, but rather structures the trend movement, with its respective corrections, whether in uptrends or downtrends.

This completes the analysis we have been doing throughout this book. We already know the causes that form price trends: the processes of accumulation and distribution. We have been categorising and disaggregating these structures and analysing the different events that occur in them. Now it is time to see what the price does when it is in a trend (bullish or bearish), the corrections it makes, and what the main objectives we can look for are.

As I said, Elliott Wave Theory is very broad, and many books could be written about it. In this chapter, we are only going to focus on certain aspects that have been useful to me in my day-to-day trading. All of this will be done in a very practical way, so as not to forget that this is just another tool offered by technical analysis to label impulses, corrections and target zones.

Before we begin, both Elliott Wave Theory and VSA complement each other perfectly. They are not mutually exclusive, quite the contrary. Their combination is the key to all of this.

3.1 ORGANISING THE IMPULSES

So far, we have seen how the different structures that precede impulses develop. Now, let's focus on the impulses themselves and their corrections.

After a process of accumulation or distribution, the price begins an upward or downward impulse, which in turn contains impulses and corrections. Impulses do not occur in a straight line, but rather both supply and demand must continuously test whether the opposing force is present in the market and, if so, attempt to absorb or eliminate it.

The price, as we already know, always follows the line of least resistance. It is a basic law. Just as water always flows along the path that is easiest for it to find, the price does the same. Until it reaches a dam that slows its advance, as we have already seen.

Well, Elliott Wave Theory structures bullish impulses into five waves. Since the market is fractal, each of these five waves can be subdivided into another five waves. In this way, there are different degrees.

In turn, these five waves usually have three impulsive waves (I-III-V) and two corrective waves (II-IV).

If we have an upward impulse (I), it is followed by a corrective impulse (II), then another upward impulse (III), its corrective impulse (IV), and the higher-degree impulse ends with a final upward wave (V).

Then, another corrective impulse of a higher degree will begin. In turn, corrective impulses (II-IV) can be subdivided into smaller waves (ABC / ABCDE).

This is again like Russian matryoshka dolls, where each doll contains a smaller one, which in turn contains another smaller one.

In summary, everything we have just discussed can be seen in the following image. There are thousands of Elliott diagrams on the Internet if you want to be more purist, but here is a practical example of a real asset, the NASDAQ100, during the 2009 financial crisis.

Chart 20: Elliot waves count (NASDAQ100)

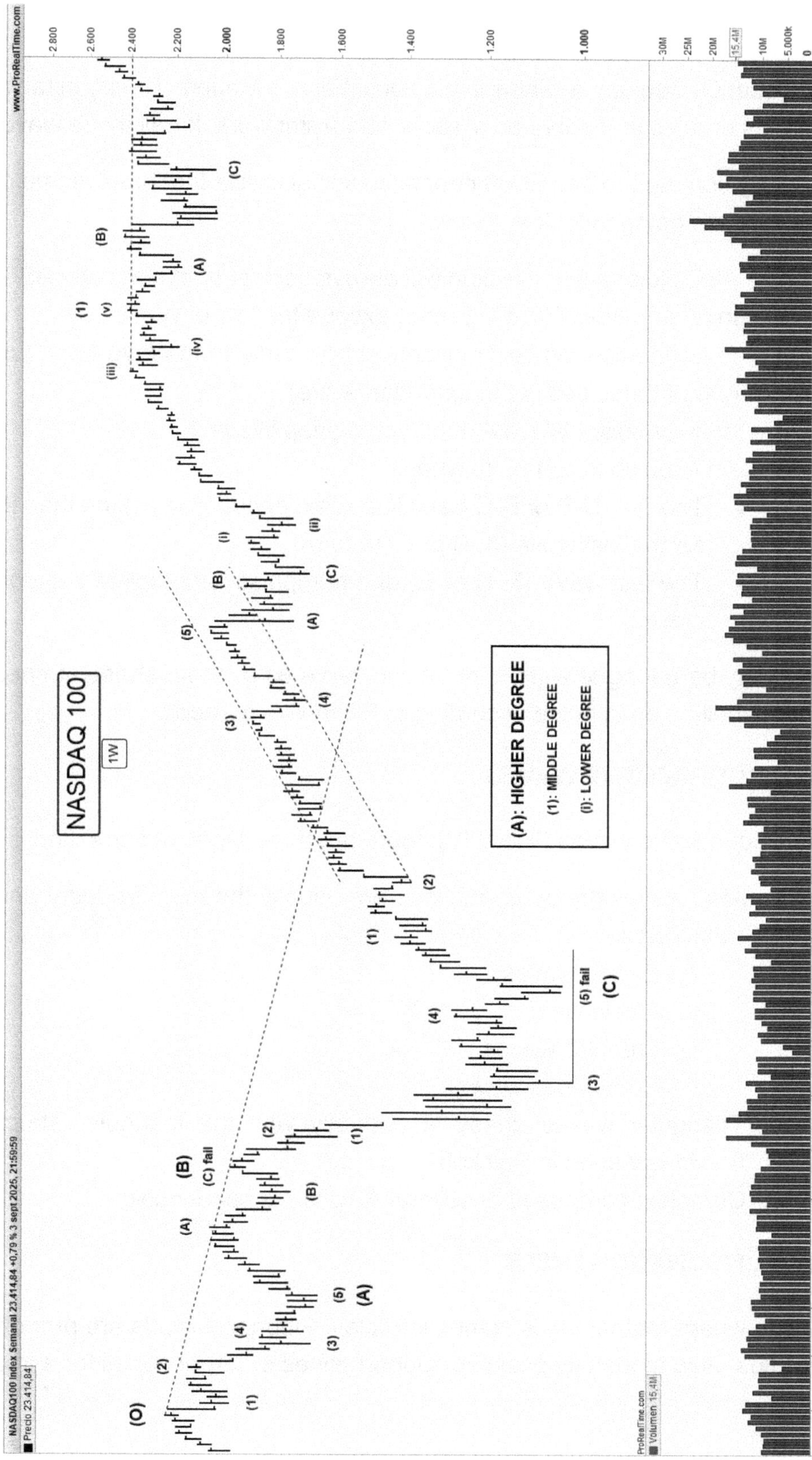

3.1.1 REGLAS GENERALES

As Óscar G. Cagigas explains in his book, Elliott's Modern Theory establishes a series of rules that serve as a 'regulatory framework' for all these waves.

It is very common to see Elliott counts on social media that break some of the rules we are going to look at below:

1. ABC Rule: any correction will always consist of at least one ABC.
2. In an impulse, Wave 2 cannot exceed the low of Wave 1.
3. In an impulse, Wave 3 must never be shorter than Wave 1 or 5 (unless one of these two is the extended wave).
4. In an impulse, Wave 4 must not overlap Wave 1.
5. An impulse is complete when:
    - The 2-4, O-B or B-D trend line is exceeded in less time than it took for the last wave (5, C or E) to form.
    - The last wave (5, C or E) of the impulse is completely undone at closing.

This may be a tongue twister, but it can serve as a 'cheat sheet' or checklist when labelling an impulse according to Elliott Wave Theory.

3.1.2 CORRECTIVE WAVES

Within corrective waves (II and IV), there are three types of corrections:

- ABC waves: these corrections are usually the most frequent and are classified as:
    - Zigzag waves
    - Flat waves
    - Irregular waves
    - Continuous waves
- Triangular waves: these fit perfectly with the triangular structures previously seen in Wyckoff.
- Complex: composed of several ABC wave sequences.

3.1.3 FIBONACCI LEVELS

This is where mathematics comes into play. Fibonacci levels are proportions or ratios used to identify possible support zones or target zones for a trend.

For your information: the Fibonacci sequence is a series of numbers where each number is the sum of the previous two (1, 1, 2, 3, 5, 8, 13, 21, etc.). This sequence gives rise to the various ratios of interest in technical analysis (24% / 38% / 62% / 100% / 127% / 168%...).

Note: 50% is not a number in the Fibonacci series, but it is also often used among these ratios of interest.

3.2 KEY ASPECTS

Now that we know that impulses are subdivided into waves and that these waves have specific characteristics, let us extract what I consider to be the most important aspects of Elliott Wave Theory.

3.2.1 WAVE 1 (IMPULSIVE)

After a Wyckoff accumulation or distribution process, the impulse in the form of Wave 1 begins from the lowest or highest point of this process.

This is the first impulse that goes against the trend to the left of the Wyckoff structure.

It consists of five smaller waves.

3.2.2 WAVE 2 (CORRECTIVE)

After an initial attempt at rebellion against the main trend (Wave 1), the price corrects this impulse.

This Wave 2 is characterised by being composed of three ABC waves, normally in a corrective zigzag pattern.

Often, this Wave 2 coincides with the substructure that occurs in the form of JAC/BUEC in accumulation processes (or in the form of BTI/BOI in distribution processes).

3.2.3 WAVE 3 (IMPULSIVE)

Normally, this wave has the longest price and time range of all of them. In turn, the wave will increase its speed each time it moves further away from Wave 1, thus reaching cruising speed. Therefore, it is the best wave to trade, as the risk is limited by being in the middle of the impulse and the profit can be very lucrative.

One of the metrics I usually use is that Wave 3 can reach a range equal to 162% of Wave 1. That is, Wave 3 = 162% Wave 1.

3.2.4 WAVE 4 (CORRECTIVE)

After a substantial price movement in the form of Wave 3, the price takes a break.

It usually lasts longer than Wave 2 and tends to alternate in type. If Wave 2 was an ABC wave, Wave 4 is usually complex.

3.2.5 WAVE 5 (IMPULSIVE)

Wave 5 is the last wave of the major impulse. When we see that the impulse has already made four waves (two impulsive and two corrective), a final upward Wave 5 could form as the end of the entire impulse.

This wave is the one that, before forming, has the most information, since we already have the other four waves developed.

The metric I usually use is that Wave 5 has a projection equal to that of Wave 1. That is, Wave 5 = Wave 1 in price and, sometimes, in time.

Another interesting metric to look at is that Wave 5 is also usually equal to 32% / 50% / 62% of Wave 3 projected from the start of Wave 5.

In some markets, such as commodities, this wave is usually the extended wave, i.e. the longest.

If Wave 5 does not exceed the high of Wave 3, a Wave 5 failure will occur, which has very negative repercussions, as the subsequent correction tends to undo the entire higher-degree impulse.

Sometimes, this Wave 5 has terminal pattern characteristics. This means that it usually takes the form of a contracting triangular structure with a bullish bias (if the trend is bullish) or bearish bias (if the trend is bearish). The result of this structure is an exhaustion in the final movement of the impulse, which sees the other side of the force (supply or demand) slowing down the price.

3.2.6 HEADS-UP

So far, this is what I consider to be the most important aspect of Elliott Wave Theory.

In my experience, you must be very meticulous when counting Elliott waves (always following the rules), and personally, I prefer to label corrections rather than impulses.

In daily trading, Elliott Wave Theory is a perfect complement to the Wyckoff methodology.

As the master would say: Wyckoff and Elliott, working together!

4. STUDY CASES

Now comes the most enjoyable part of the entire document: the practical cases.

To show you all the progress we have made in this book, we have looked at the following concepts, from least to most technically complex:

1. Main players in the market.
2. Bar chart.
3. Support, resistance and trend lines.
4. Market fractality.
5. Line of least resistance.
6. The law of supply and demand.
7. The law of cause and effect.
8. The law of effort vs. result.
9. The eight bars of strength in VSA.
10. The eight bars of weakness in VSA.
11. Accumulation and distribution processes.
12. The phases of Wyckoff structures.
13. Types of structures.
14. The nine tests of Wyckoff (strength)
15. The nine tests of Wyckoff (weakness)
16. Basic principles of Elliott Wave Theory.

Spectacular, isn't it? Whether you already knew about stock market concepts or had no idea about anything, I hope that, at this point, you know how to read the language of the market perfectly. Come on!

However, if you think that's the case, I have some bad news. This book can be useful as long as you put everything in it into practice. Practice makes perfect, and I don't mean you should start trading like a madman. I mean you should sit down in front of a screen, open the chart and start reading bar by bar what the price is doing.

In my opinion, this book contains everything you need to start deciphering the market on your own. It's not easy at first, but with time and a good mentor, if possible, you'll get there.

That said, this chapter is what I would have liked to find in many books when I started out in the world of VSA.

Practical examples. That's what I was looking for in all the technical analysis books that were based on reading charts using price and volume.

In most texts, I only found theory and schematic examples of price movements. That's one of the reasons why I've given up using this type of image in this book. Conceptually, they are very good; you get all the information at a glance. However, when it comes down to it, the market bears little resemblance to those books where all the impulses and corrections are idyllic and without delays.

So, what will you find in this chapter? The answer is clear, isn't it? Well, practical exercises.

This will always follow the same formula.

I will list the case studies, and at the beginning of each one there will be an untagged bar chart.

This chart is what you should use for your notes. It is your chart, and you can draw on it whatever you think the market is doing.

I just want you to identify the following on this chart:

1. Key levels of support and resistance.
2. Main trend lines.
3. Strength, weakness and test bars.
4. (Re)accumulation and/or (re)distribution structures.
5. Label all events and guidelines for the identified structures.

The solution, from my perspective of viewing the markets, will follow, after a detailed description of all the price movements in the chart.

If you are able to identify all of this in the chart, in the long run and with a lot of trial and error, I am sure you will be able to understand the language of the market.

Ready? Grab a pen and paper and let's get practising.

Case 1: Enphase Energy

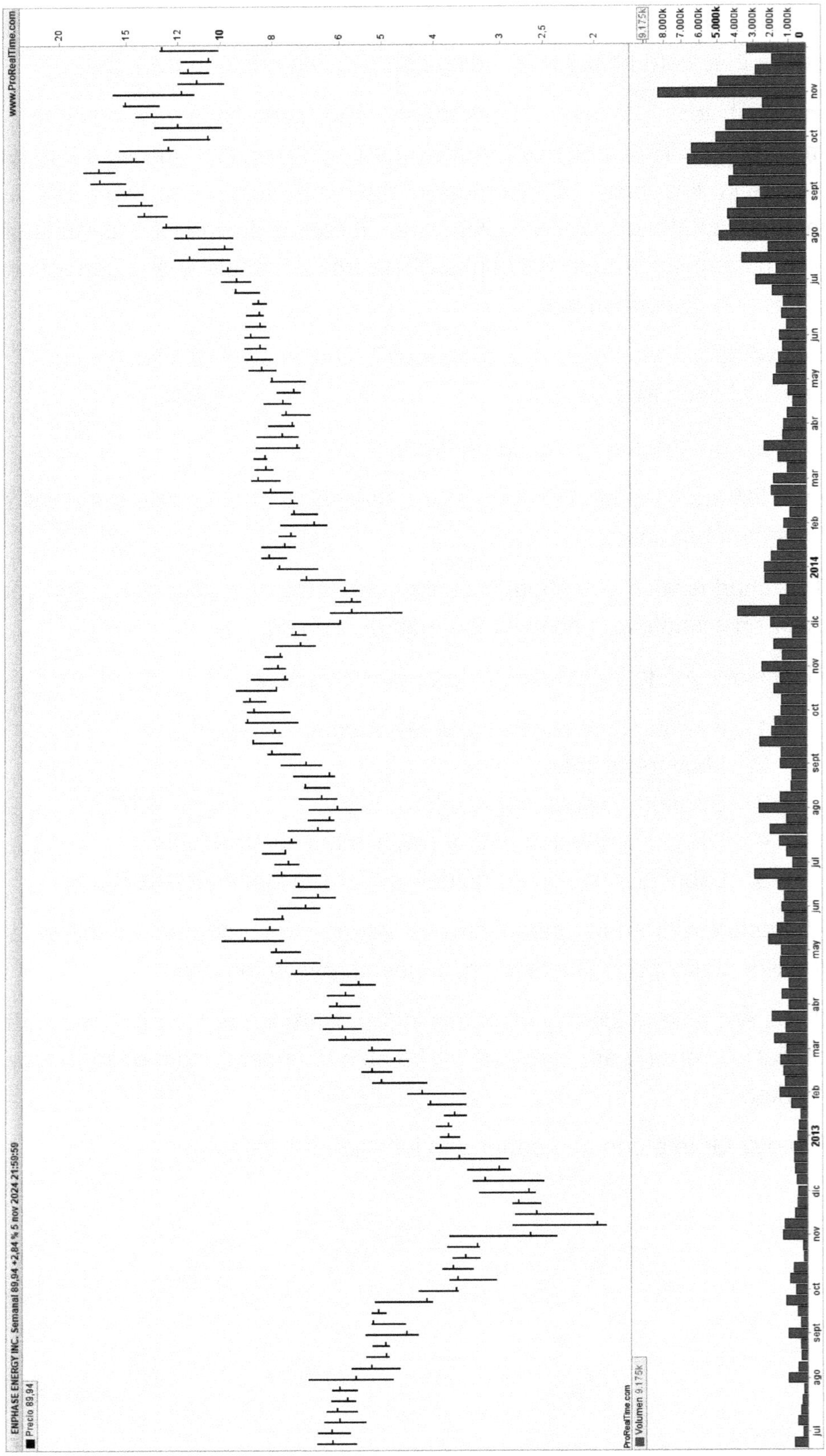

Let's look at the first case study: the weekly chart for Enphase Energy.

From left to right, we see a pronounced downtrend structured in a bearish channel. Weakness bars abound, as is normal. Every time the price hits the bottom, demand appears to slow the price and bring it back up to the top.

There comes a point when the value breaks the base of the channel and wide-range, high-volume bearish bars occur. These situations usually coincide with oversold levels in the market, so you must be alert to possible reversals. That is how it happened. After that reversal, the price broke the bearish channel at the top and a V-shaped reversal occurred.

The price then followed a flawless bullish channel. When the time came, the value accelerated its rise and expanded the top of the channel (overbought level), and the bullish bar closed far from the highs and with climatic volume. We now have a potential BC. The price then broke through the base of the bullish channel and successfully tested the break. We would have the AR and ST there.

In turn, it seems that a support level is forming around $5.50, a level to watch. From there, the price followed a slight downward channel, where we see bars of strength at the base and weakness at the top, as is to be expected.

In a show of courage, the stock breaks through the bottom of the channel and extends the support at $5.50. However, it closes above that level with a wide-range bearish bar, climatic volume (the highest to date) and a close far from the lows. Here we would have potential strength in a hypothetical Phase C in the form of a TSO.

Afterwards, the price is able to break the internal diagonal (minor creek) and attack the upper part of the horizontal structure with a downward bias. After several failed attempts, supply withdraws each time the price falls, another sign of strength. Inevitably, it breaks the upper part and tests it several times, successfully (BUEC).

Finally, the value rises, structured in an upward channel, until supply re-enters in a new zone, where it slows down again.

Case 2: Enphase Energy (Solution)

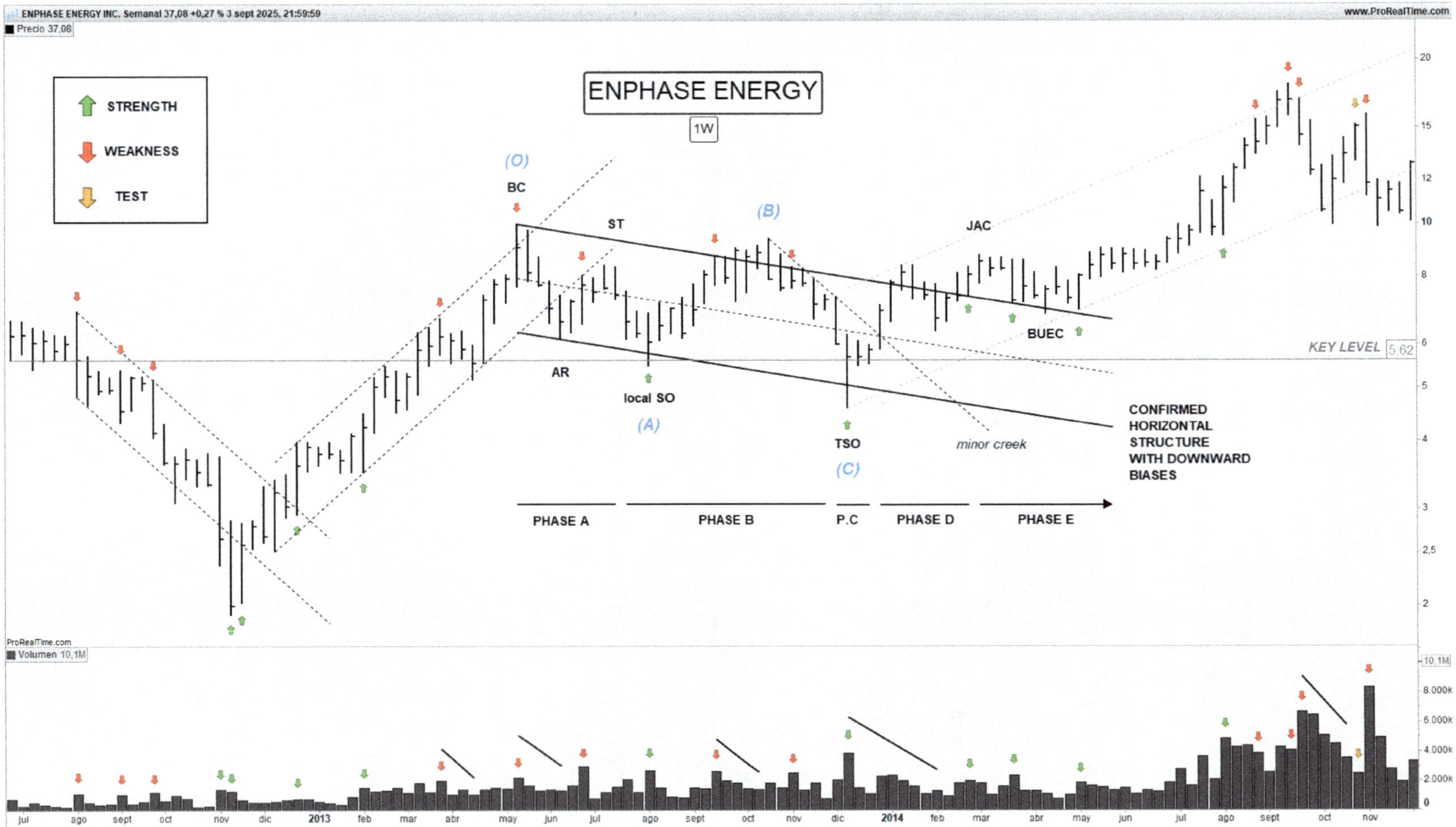

Case 2: Bitcoin / USD

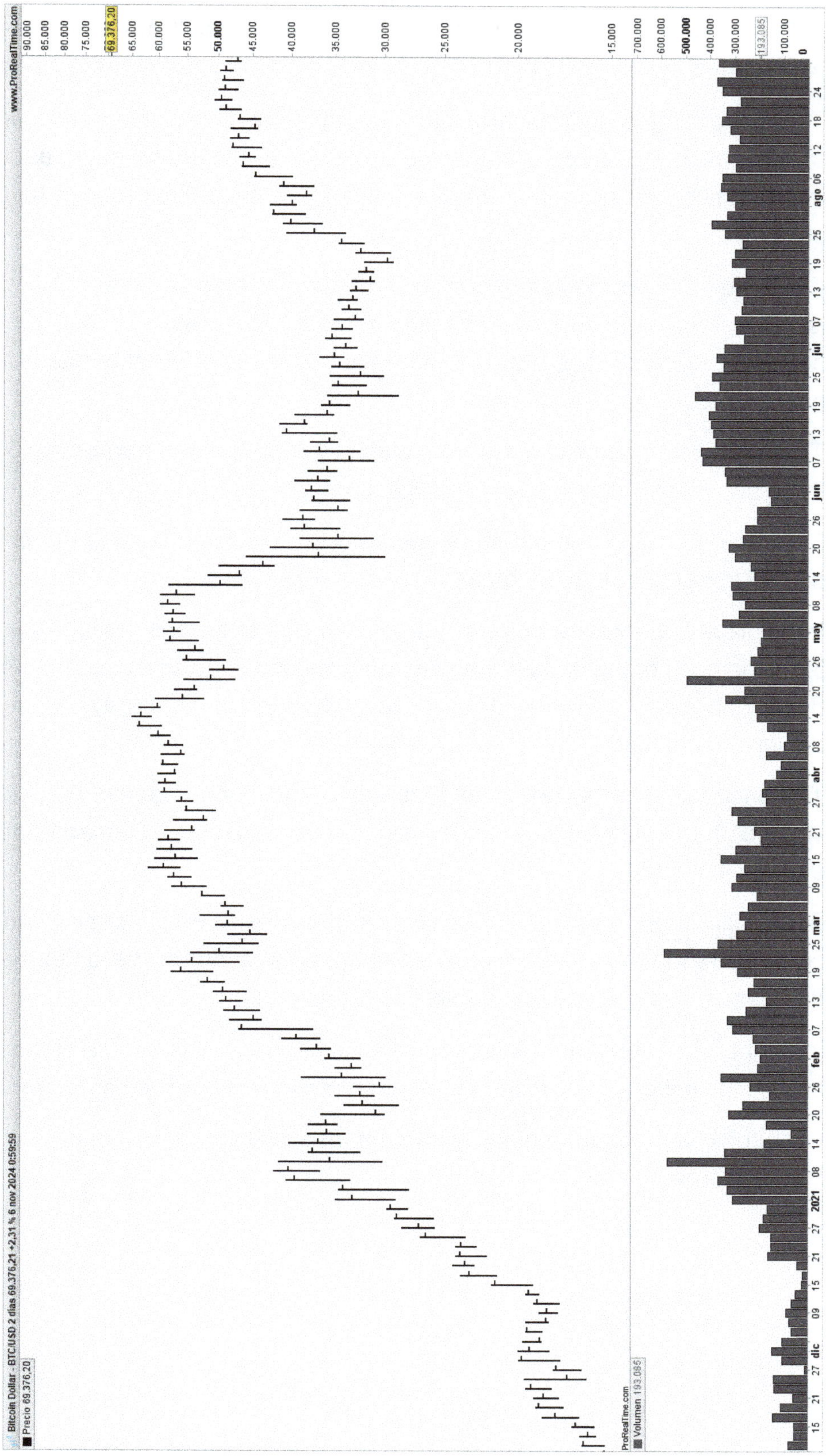

Let's go back to those crazy months of the Bitcoin bull run after the 2020 halving.

The price enters a flawless uptrend, with two contracting triangular re-accumulation structures that resolve upwards. In these, we can clearly see demand supporting the price at the bottom and supply retreating. Textbook stuff.

Once the price begins its upward journey, supply starts to appear. A first sign is that the highs are no longer as high and vigorous as before. In fact, the price begins to lose impulse, and volume dries up as the price attempts to make new highs.

There comes a point when the triangulation that the price is performing begins to be apparent, in the form of ending action.

Finally, Phase C of the structure occurs with an LPSY, causing the price to break strongly through the base.

Immediately afterwards, demand comes into play and stops the fall. The price tests the base of the broken triangle again and it can be seen that the volume does not follow (volume divergences). Everything is ready for a new downward impulse.

The price falls sharply again until there is a wide-range bearish bar, climatic volume, in the support zone and closing far from the lows. Demand has said enough is enough.

The price then remains above the key support level, forming another contracting triangle. In it, we can see bars of strength at the bottom and a decrease in volume as it advances (drying up of supply).

In a final attempt to break through the support, the price fails (Phase C), breaks the minor creek and the upper part of the structure, which it later tests.

Everything is ready for a new upward impulse, as indeed happened.

Case 2: Bitcoin / USD (Solution)

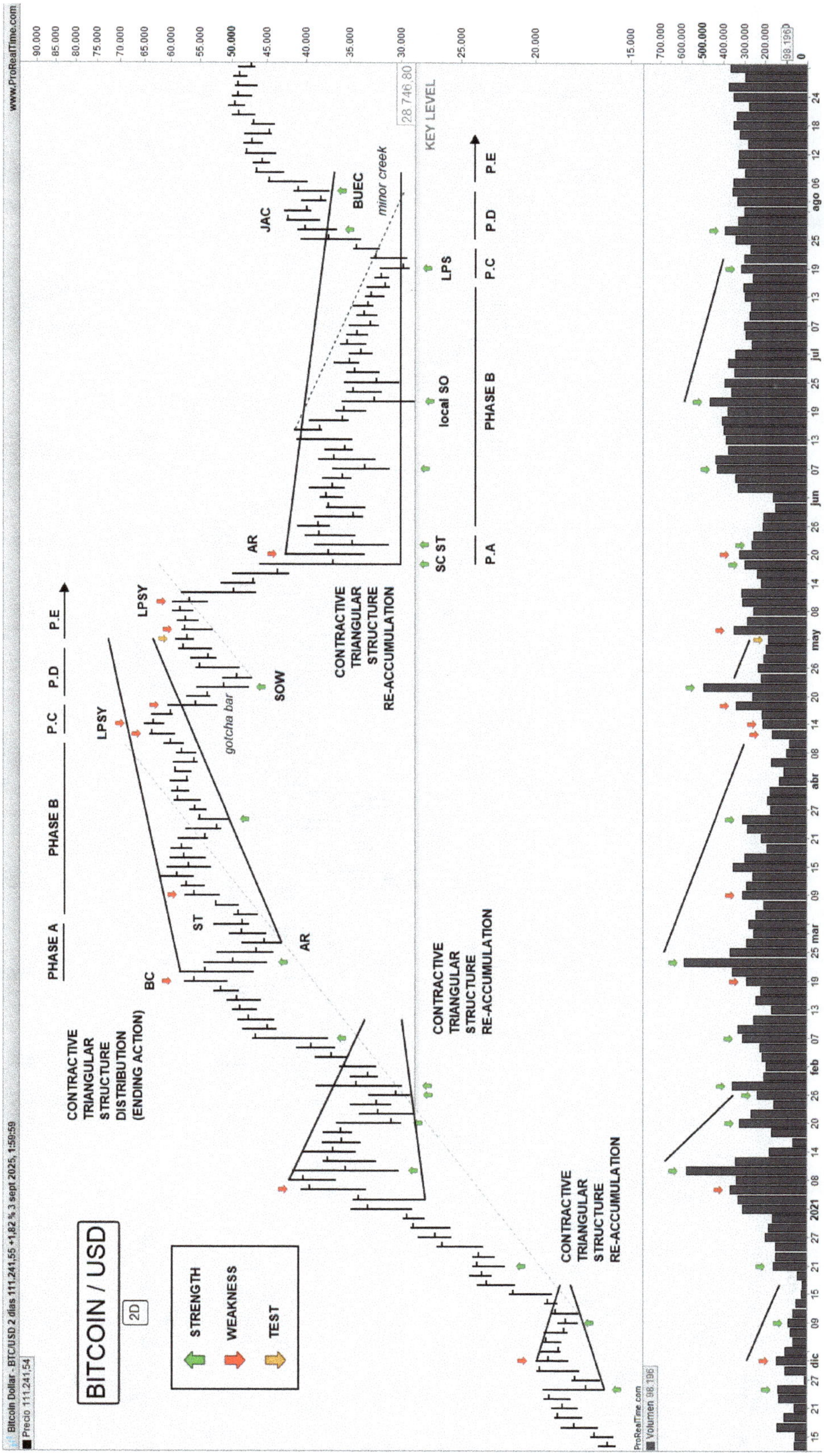

Case 3: Micron Technologies

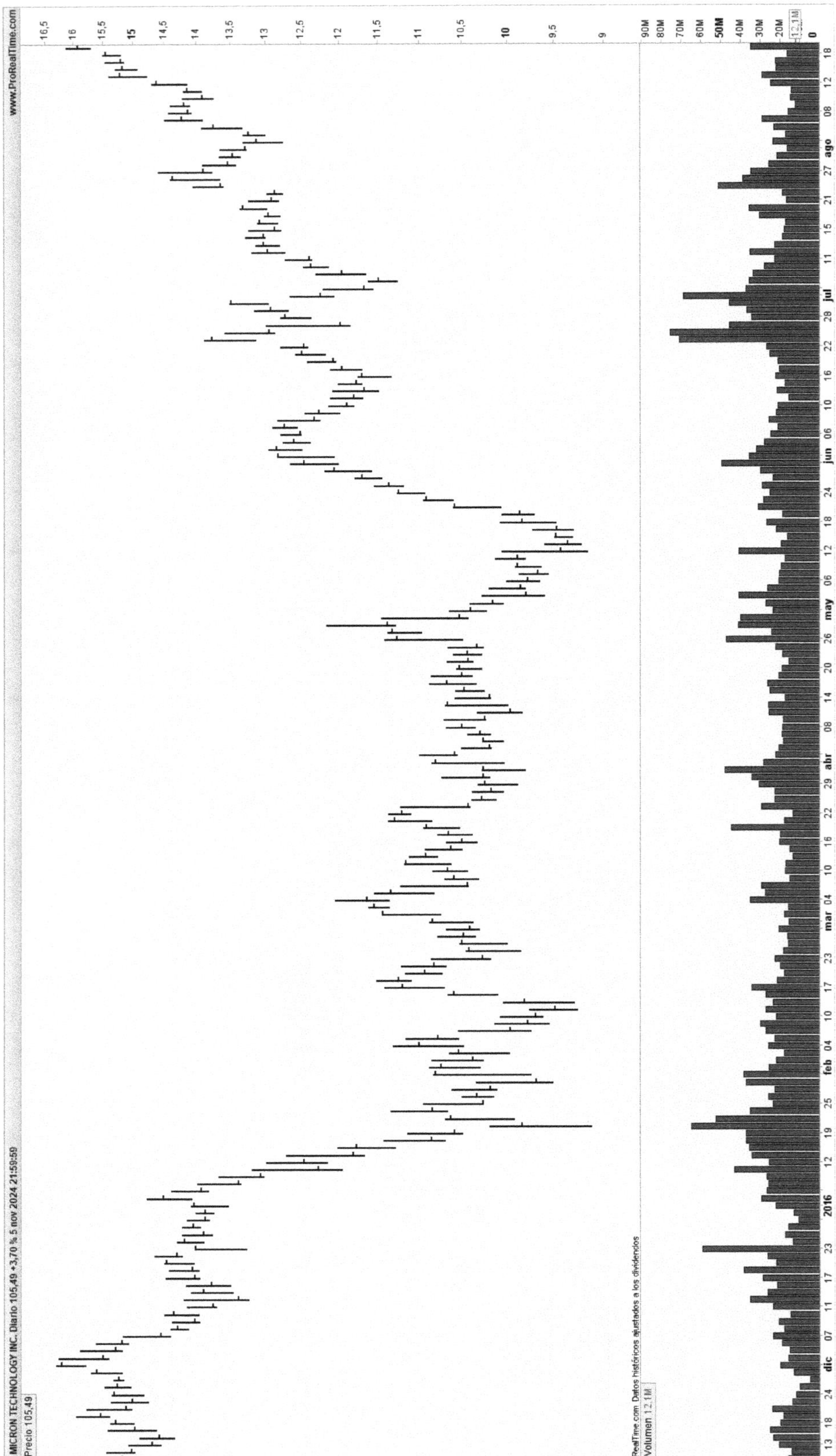

Now that we have some experience under our belts, let's take it a step further. Let's put Wyckoff's 9 tests into practice.

The chart is very interesting.

We start with an underlying downtrend. In the middle, there is a horizontal redistribution structure. The value continues to fall until demand for the price occurs and a horizontal structure is formed. The price continues to advance in the development of the structure and breaks the main downtrend line. However, it falls back below it and makes a final test of the bottom of the structure in the form of an LPS.

Finally, the price rises, but supply enters again. This is when a re-accumulation substructure in the form of a BUEC occurs (something very typical in the market). In Elliott's jargon, the price corrected the impulse initiated in the LPS with an irregular flat wave (strong B, denoting strength).

After retesting the bottom of the substructure, which is also the top of the already broken higher-degree structure, the price begins its upward flight.

Let's run it through Wyckoff's 9 strength tests, answering his questions:

1. Has the price reached the bearish target or has the price previously made a substantial downward move? - Correct
2. Is there evidence that the price is being held back by demand? - Correct
3. Is there bullish activity? That is, does volume expand when it rises and retreat when it falls? - Correct
4. Has the downtrend been broken? - Indeed
5. Are there higher lows? - Correct
6. Are there higher highs? - Correct
7. Does the asset have relative strength? – Certainly
8. Has a base been formed? – Correct
9. Is the estimated upside potential greater than the downside potential? – Most likely.

With all this in mind, we can say that the probability of the price rising from now on is very high.

Case 3: Micron Technologies (Solution)

Case 4: Microsoft

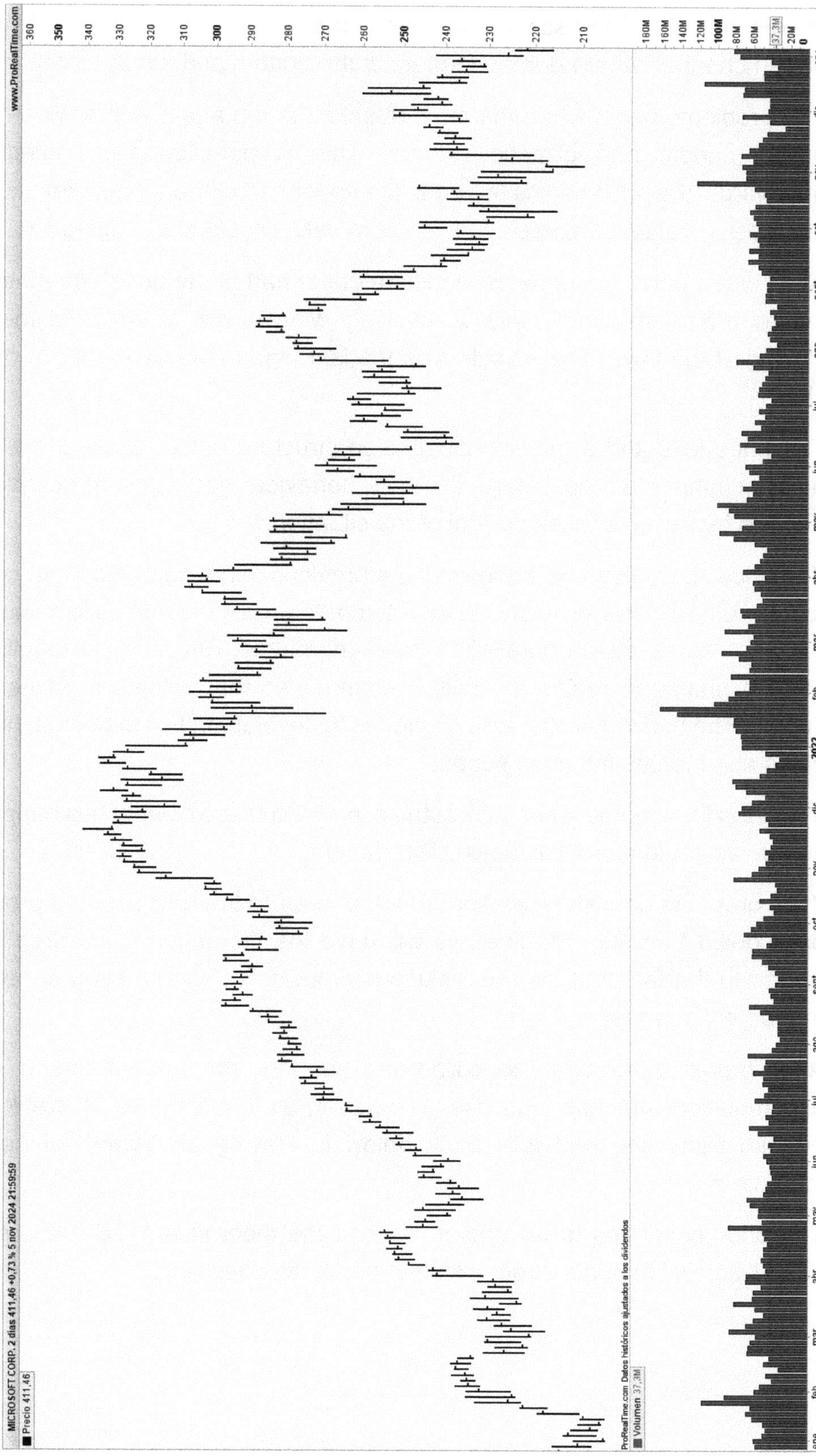

Microsoft's turn. The asset in question starts the chart by forming a flawless bullish channel, where demand enters at the bottom and supply at the top.

The problems begin when the price attacks the top again with a wide-range bullish candle and climatic volume. This is pure supply. Immediately afterwards, the price begins to 'climb' the upper part of the bullish channel with decreasing volume. In these cases, alarm bells should start ringing.

At a certain point, the price expands the upper part of the bullish channel and leaves a bearish candle, with a relatively wide range, climatic volume and closing at the lows. That candle was the last high made by the stock on the chart.

The price falls and a minor redistribution structure occur, causing the main bullish channel to break. Here, the price behaviour has changed completely, and the bears have taken control of the situation.

The price slows down at the lows of the previous minor correction and begins to form a horizontal structure. In an attempt to regain the lost bullish channel, the price forms bullish bars with ultra-high volume. Effort vs. no result. The price is unable to regain the bullish channel, so that volume must be pure supply. The horizontal structure continues to develop and as expected, breaks down and pierces the main support.

If we stop for a moment and look at the complete picture of what has happened so far, we could see a full-blown H&S pattern.

If we draw the bearish projection from the head to the neckline and project it back down from the neckline, we will have the theoretical price drop level. Added to the fact that we are making new lows, we should keep an eye on that potential target.

After breaking through the collarbone support, the price forms a small accumulation structure and rises. However, in that impulse, it breaks the bearish trend line and falls back below it, leaving an 'island' of bearish implications.

The price continues to fall until it reaches the theoretical H&S fall target. It seems surreal that this target was met perfectly, doesn't it?

Case 4: Microsoft (Solution)

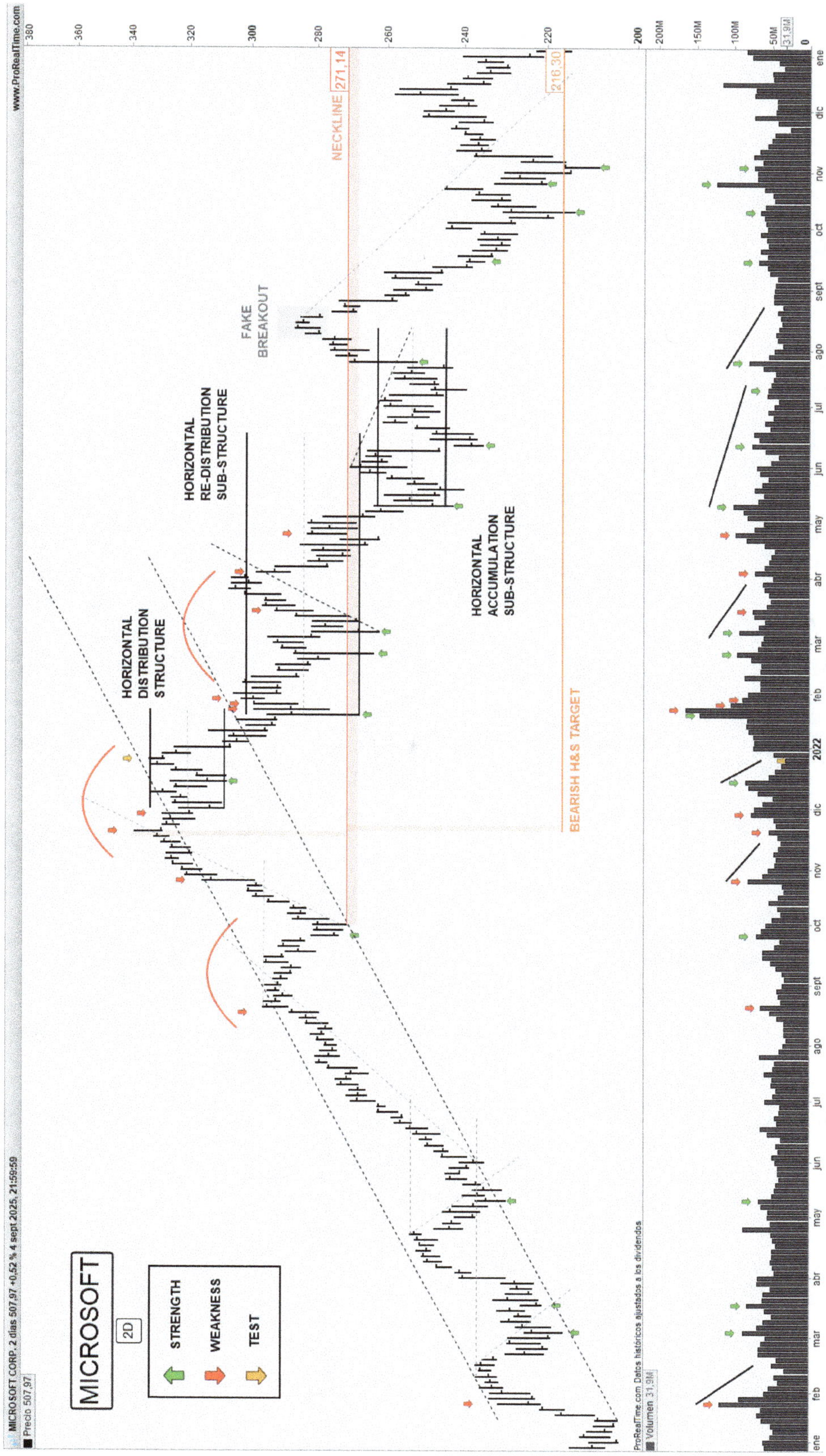

Case 5: Meta

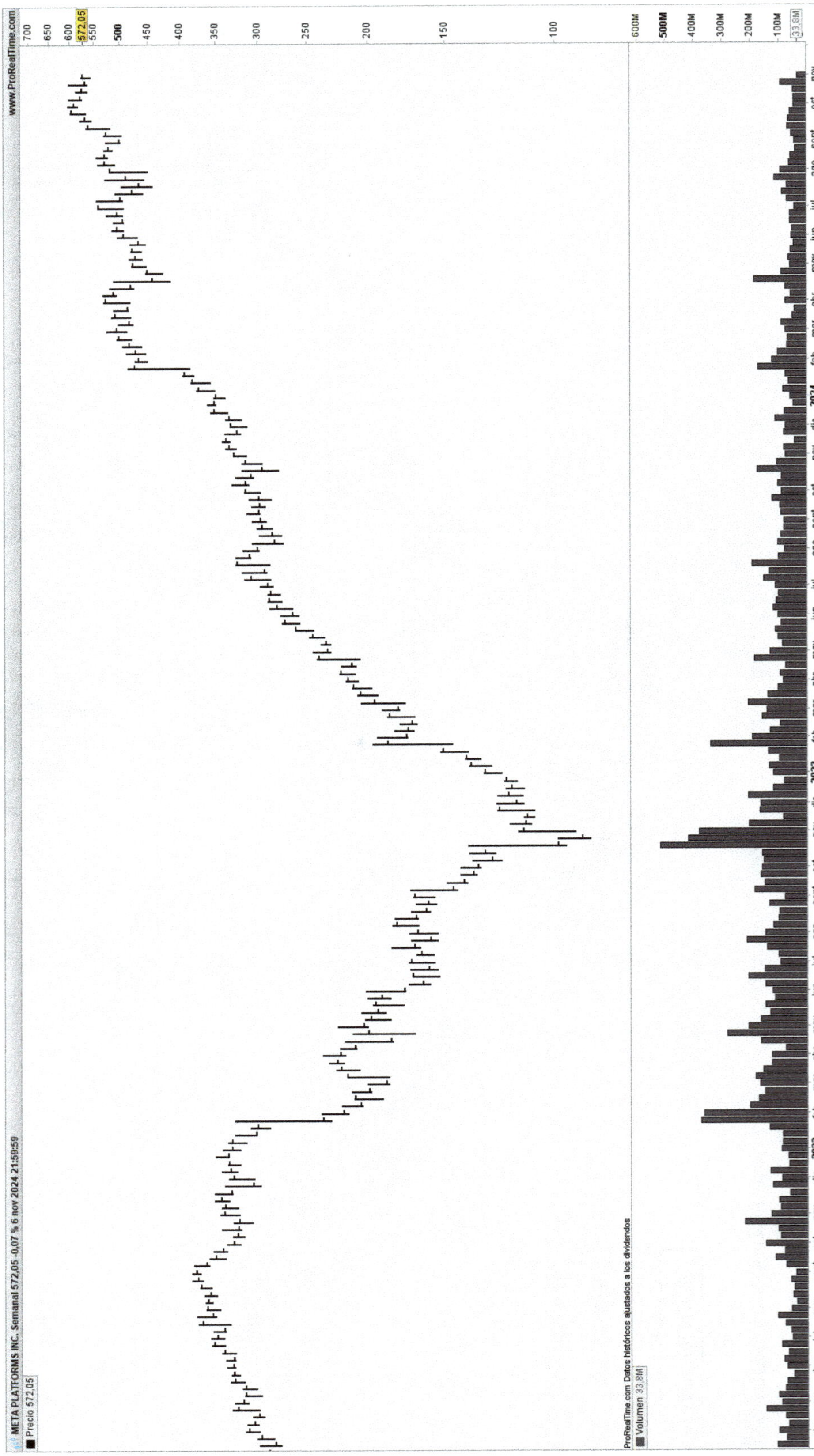

META PLATFORMS INC., Semanal 572,05 -0,07 % 6 nov 2024 21:59:59
www.ProRealTime.com
Precio 572,05
ProRealTime.com Datos históricos ajustados a los dividendos
Volumen 33,8M

Let's now look at the most spectacular strength candle on the market. The one that can change the course of history with its mere presence and power. The queen of all strength bars. Ladies and gentlemen (drum roll): bag holding!

Let's look at the following weekly chart for Meta.

You have already seen that the time frame used does not affect the analysis of price and volume. What's more, the longer the time frame, the more powerful the subsequent price movement, as it covers more bars.

The price is in a very sharp downtrend, as can be seen on the left side of the chart. In a first impulse, the price slows down and forms a first horizontal redistribution structure. Then, the value continues to fall after breaking through the lower part.

The price now follows a well-defined downward channel. When the time comes, the price breaks through the lower part of this channel, entering an extremely oversold zone.

The news about Meta is dire, with the metaverse objective, where the company is spending a fortune with little return on investment. It is precisely at this moment of selling panic that the magic happens.

After a large bearish candle with a wide range, climatic volume and closing at lows, it is followed by a bearish bar with a narrow range, climatic volume, closing relatively close to lows and in a new zone.

Stop and think about one thing here. If the previous bar has made a wide range with climatic volume, there is harmony between price and volume. However, now it makes a narrow range bar with similar volume. Is there harmony? No, right? What does VSA suggest that bar is? That all the volume is pure demand.

The price then reverses with climatic volume and recovers the lower part of the channel. As expected, numerous tests are subsequently carried out to verify that all supply has been absorbed.

The price broke through the upper part of the bearish channel and began a spectacular upward movement. All of this was motivated by a single bar: bag holding.

Case 5: Meta (Solution)

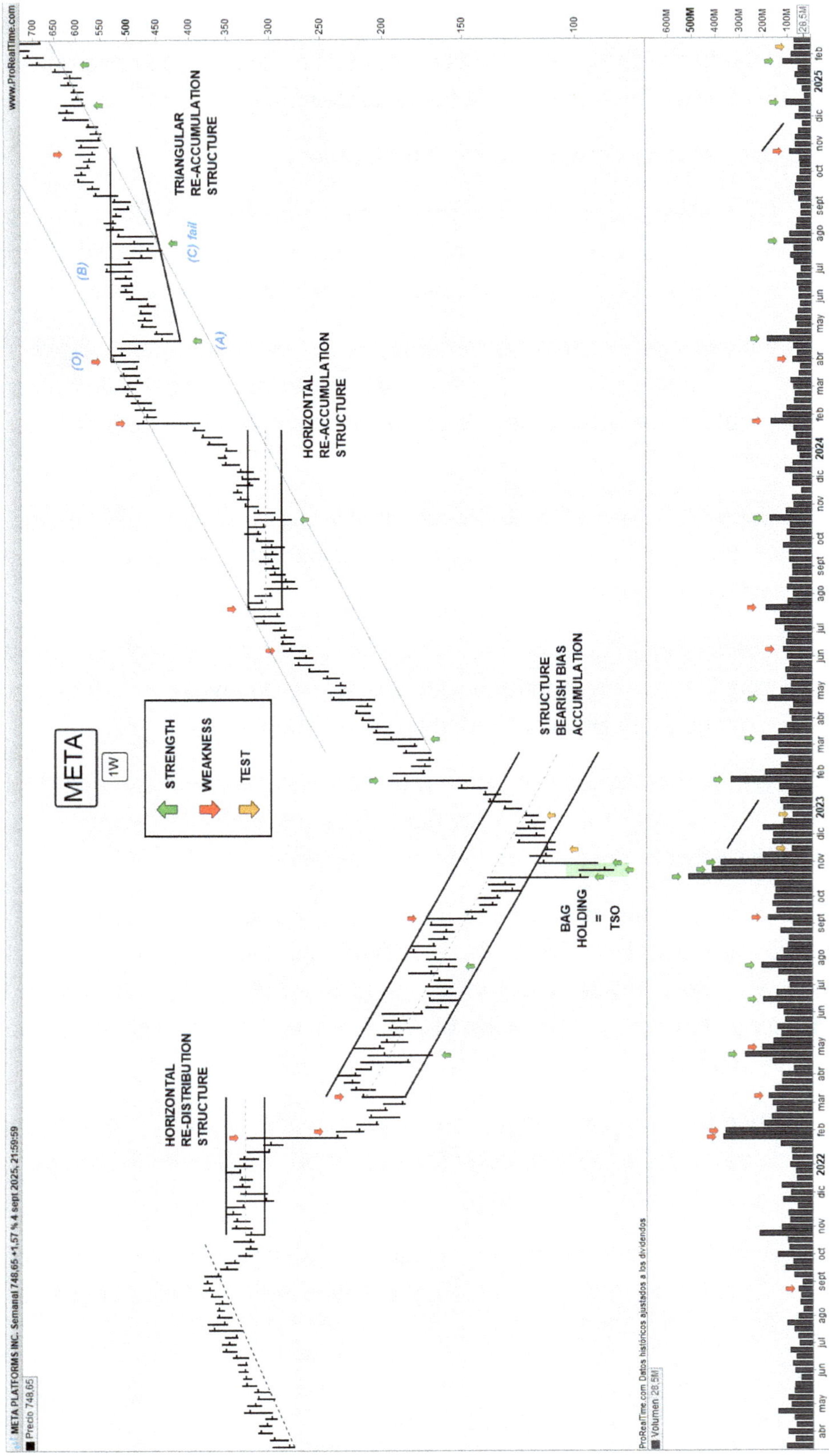

Case 6: BBVA

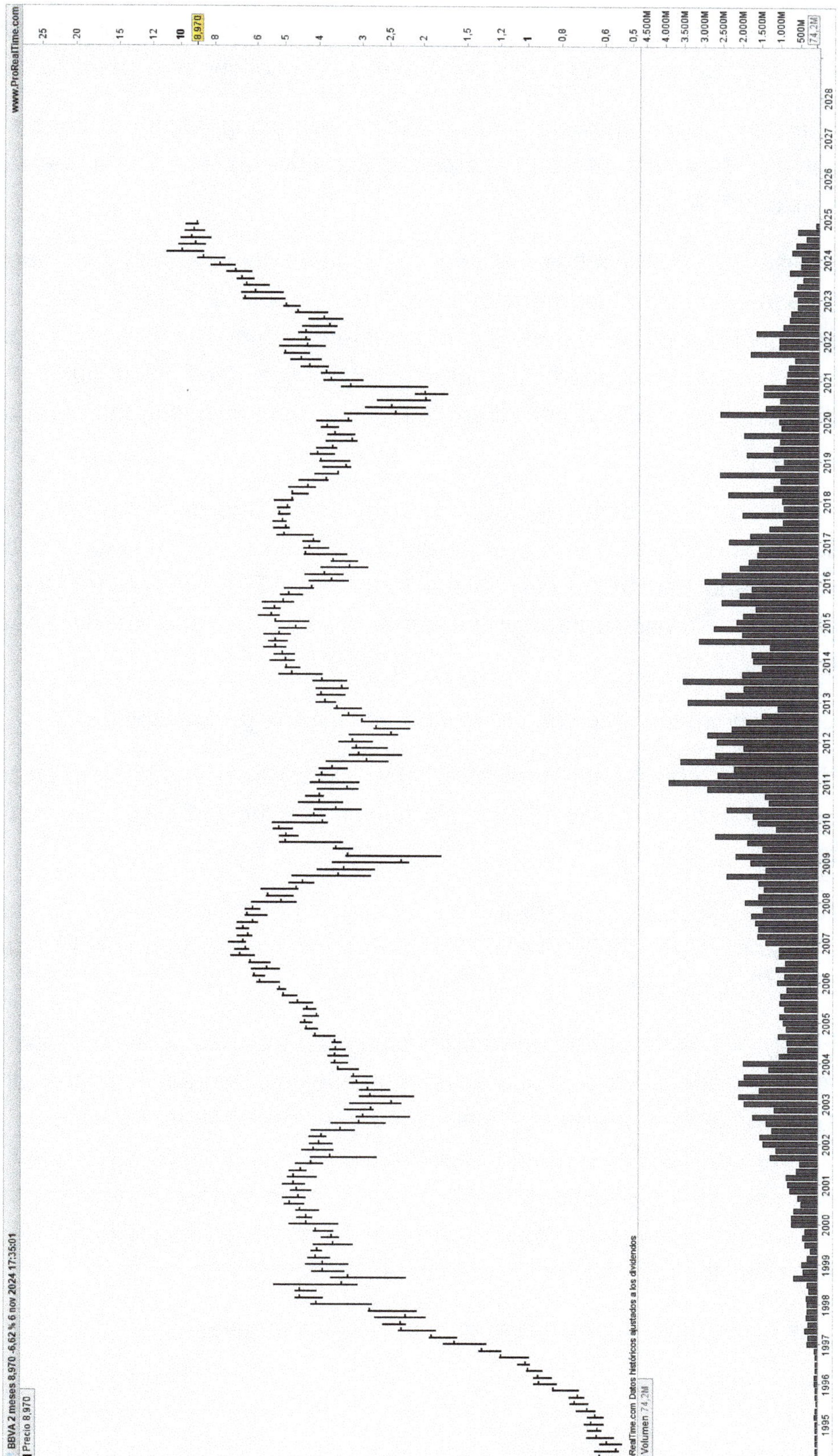
BBVA 2 meses 8,970 -6,62 % 6 nov 2024 17:35:01
www.ProRealTime.com
Precio 8,970
ProRealTime.com Datos históricos ajustados a los dividendos
Volumen 74,2M

Two-month chart, i.e. each bar contains two months of history for the security. And yet, the price and volume can be read as if nothing had changed.

The BBVA chart shows practically the entire trading history of the Spanish security. Now that we have sharpened our view, we can see a spectacular horizontal structure.

Please note that this has not been mentioned until now, and it is important. Please ensure that all the charts you use discount dividends. Every time a security pays dividends, money leaves the company's coffers, so it is worth less on the stock market. Therefore, the chart itself must automatically discount that dividend price from the y-axis, thus adjusting the chart to the dividends.

That said, the structure is not particularly novel. The price moves from one side of the structure to the other until, in Phase C, an imbalance between supply and demand occurs in the form of a TSO. From there, the price skyrockets, breaking through the top of the structure and reaching new all-time highs.

Let's now work on the chart to identify possible long-term target areas.

If we take Wave 1 (for lack of a better name) as the impulse prior to the horizontal structure, the 162% projection falls on the €21 area. That would be target 3.

Now, we move that same wave to the beginning of the new upward impulse that starts at the TSO. The 100% projection of Wave 1 from the TSO falls in the €16 zone. That would be target 2.

Finally, we focus on the upward impulse from the TSO. It seems that it has already made a Wave (I) and a Wave (II) of lesser degree. If we now plot the 162% projection of Wave (I), we get the €10 zone. If, from the start of Wave (II), we transfer Wave (I) and project it upwards, 100% of Wave (I) also falls precisely in the €10 zone. As luck would have it, that zone, without any resistance, has slowed down the price for now, leaving a target zone 1. Recently, the price has also reached target zone 2.

This is a method I often use to project possible targets.

Case 6: BBVA (Solution)

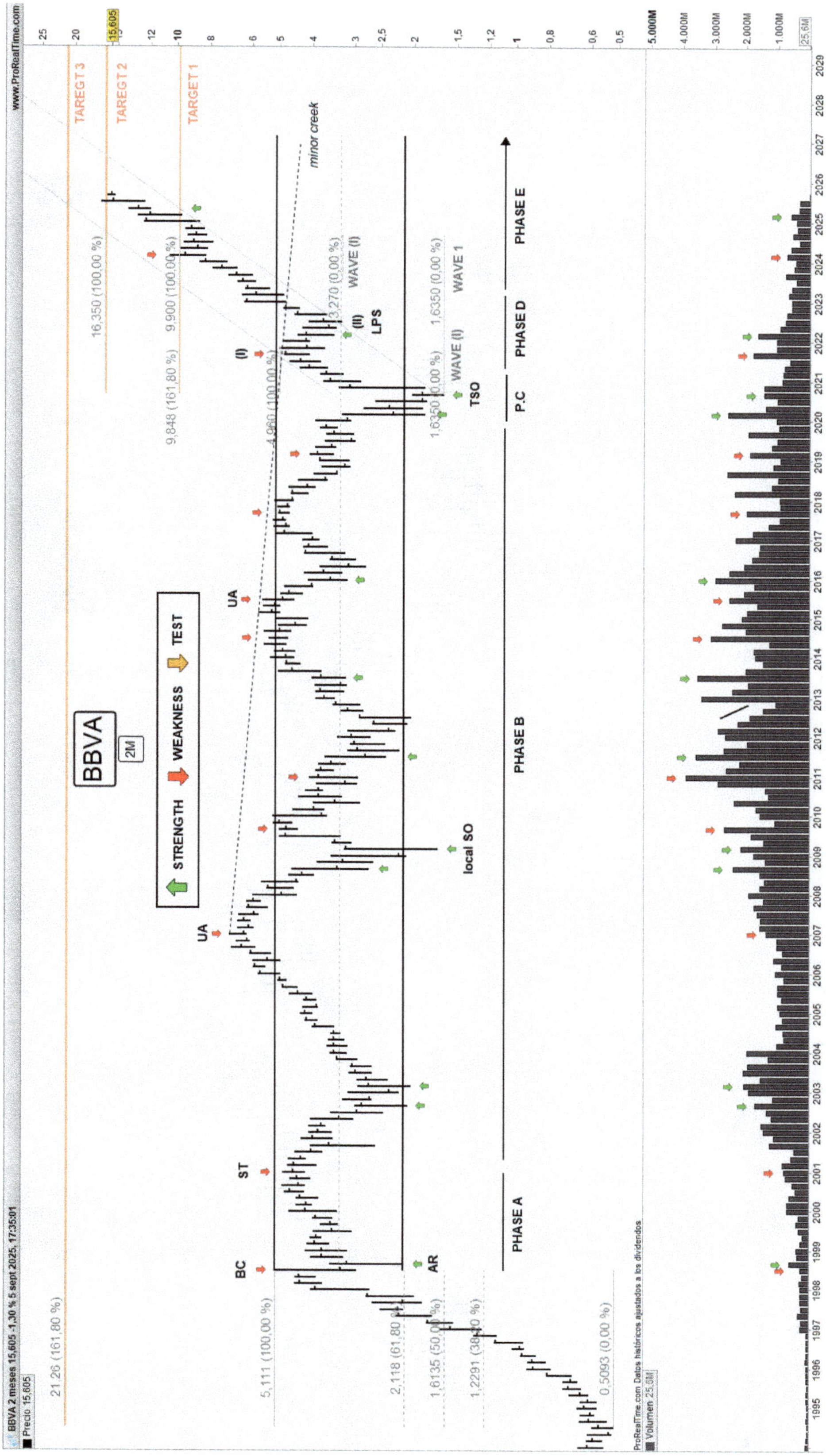

Case 7: Gold

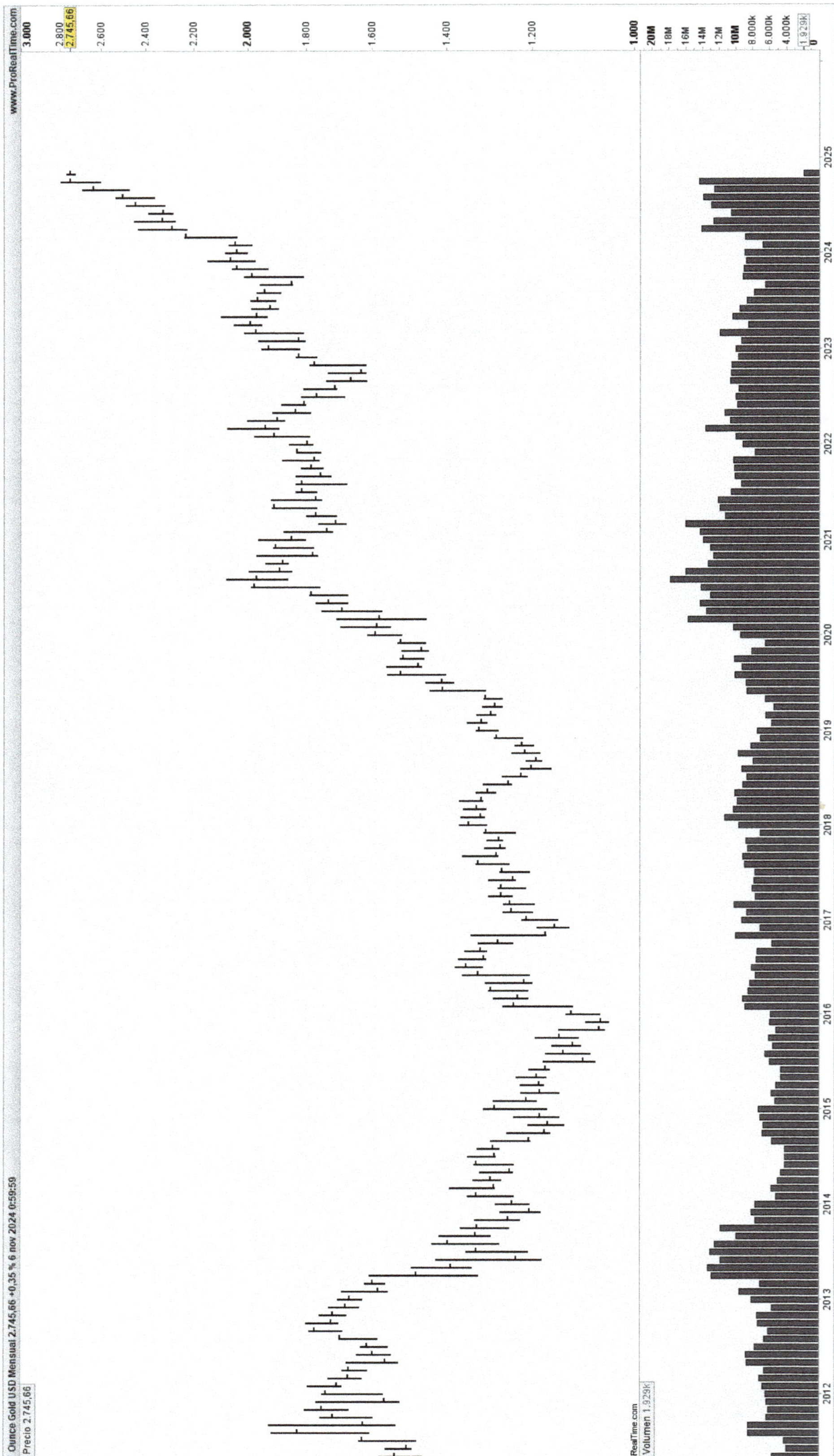

Ounce Gold USD Mensual 2.745,66 +0,35 % 6 nov 2024 0:59:59
Precio 2.745,66
www.ProRealTime.com
3.000
2.800
2.745,66
2.600
2.400
2.200
2.000
1.800
1.600
1.400
1.200
1.000
ProRealTime.com
Volumen 1.929k
20M
18M
16M
14M
12M
10M
8.000k
6.000k
4.000k
1.929k
0
2012
2013
2014
2015
2016
2017
2018
2019
2020
2021
2022
2023
2024
2025

What did you think? That this methodology was only useful for analysing stocks and crypto assets? Nothing could be further from the truth. Let's put it to the test now with one of the quintessential commodities: gold.

We could spend hours talking about this chart. Let's try to condense the entire analysis onto this page.

On the left, we have a horizontal distribution structure, with a Phase C in the form of an LPSY that does not even come close to the BC highs, denoting weakness.

The price breaks downwards and, in its bearish journey, forms a contracting triangle, bearish wedge or ending action, whatever you want to call it, formed, of course, in five ABCDE waves and with a clear decrease in volume.

The triangulation resolves upwards and once again supply comes into play, slowing down the price development. This produces another horizontal structure.

Once again, in Phase C, the price is unable to reach the minimum level of the AR, indicating strength.

The price manages to break upwards and heads for the highs of the previous horizontal distribution structure.

Once the target is reached, supply re-enters the stock, as is to be expected, and slows down the price.

Third horizontal structure that we see in just one hundred bars. This time there is an expansion in Phase B in the form of an UA (Upthrust Action). The price then breaks violently through the lower part and recovers quickly, forming a TSO in Phase C. Everything is ready to break through the upper part.

After testing the break through the upper part (see orange arrow), the price resolves upwards, reaching new historical highs.

Four structures, three horizontal and a final one in the form of a contracting triangle, in a single chart.

Personally, I really like monthly charts because they eliminate the noise of volatility from lower time frame charts. In addition, long-term targets can be detected more easily.

Case 7: Gold (Solution)

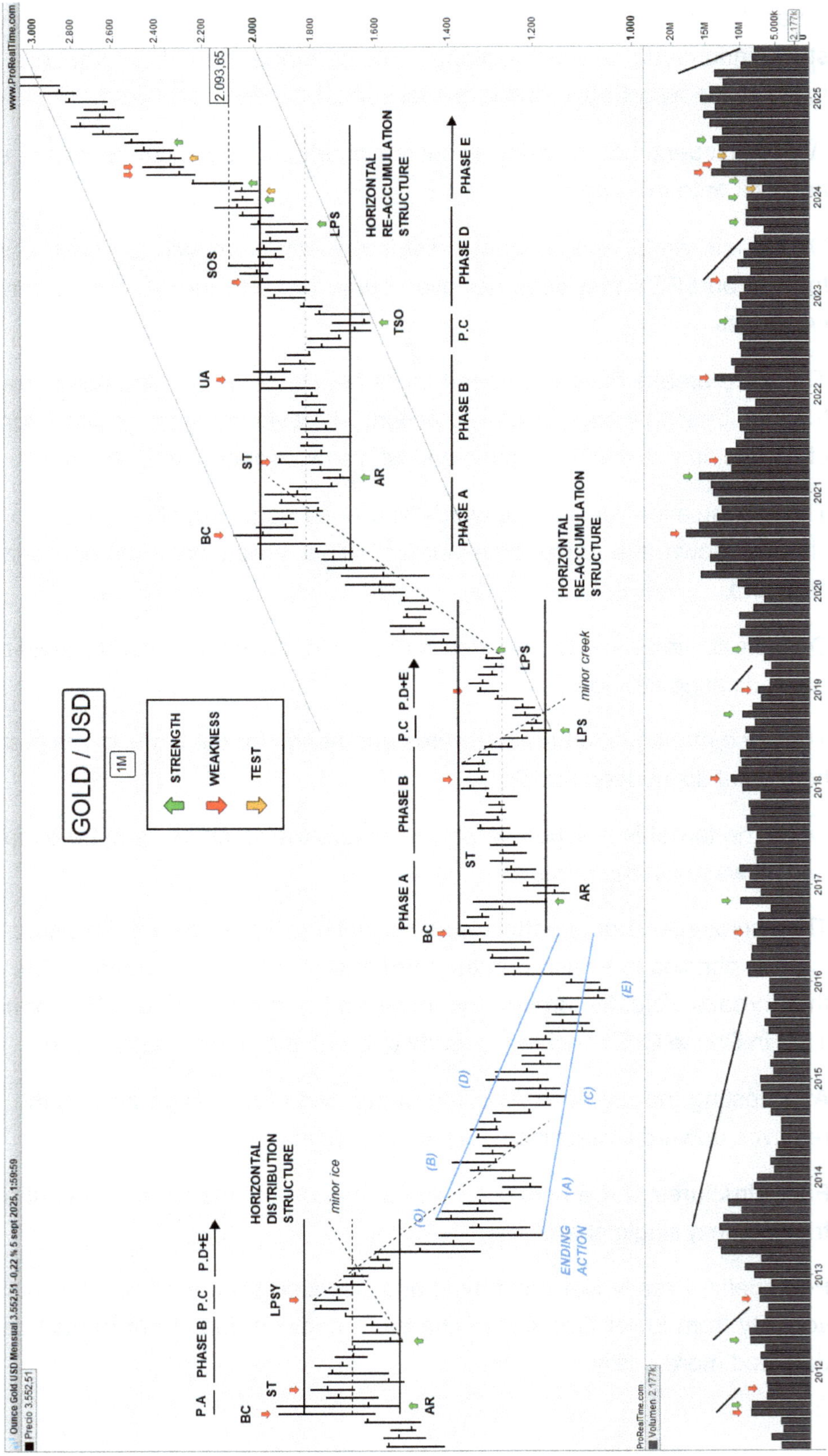

Case 8: Carvana

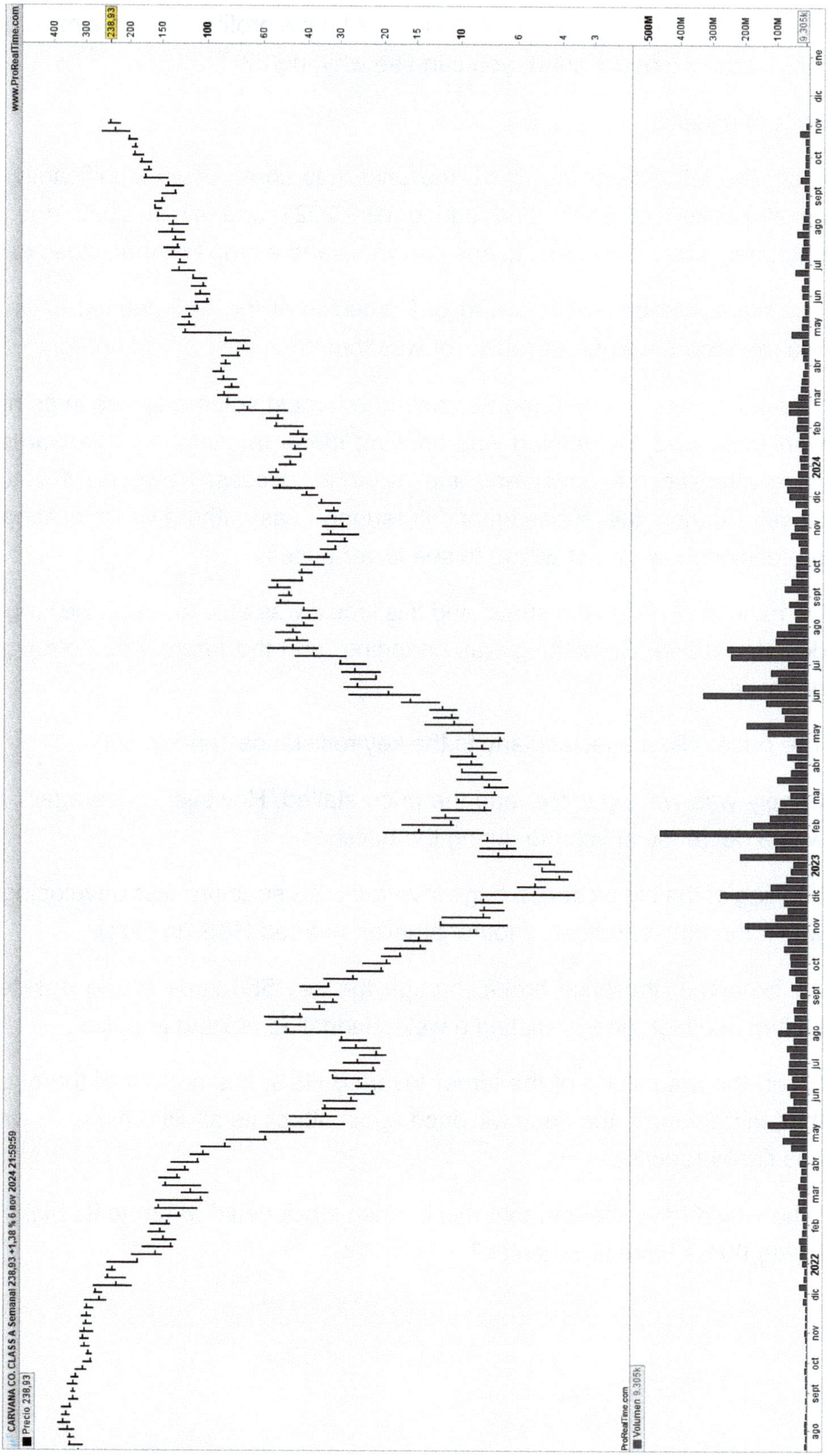

Carvana. This has been one of the assets I have profited from the most during 2023. Looking at the chart, you can see why, right?

Let's analyse it.

From the left side of the chart, the price has come down significantly. This asset peaked at $376, and during late 2021 and all of 2022, the price plummeted to around $3. No one can withstand a drop like that, close to 99%.

The price was under the sword of Damocles of the well-defined downtrend line, and there was no escape... or was there?

When the price reached the $3 zone, the largest volume spikes in its history were observed. Something was brewing there. Immediately afterwards, the price attacked the downtrend line, without success. However, if you look closely, during the subsequent fall, supply was withdrawn, indicating that professionals were not willing to see lower prices.

Demand returned to the stock, and this time it was able to break the long-term downtrend line. Something was changing, and the future was no longer so negative.

The price rallied spectacularly to the key resistance zone of $50.

Supply was waiting there, and the price stalled. However, once again, there was a decrease in volume during the declines.

Looking at the big picture, a huge inverted H&S structure was developing, and within the right shoulder, another smaller inverted H&S (in blue).

As expected, the price broke through the key $50 zone to the upside and shifted into high gear, initiating a well-channelled upward impulse.

Given the magnitude of the larger inverted H&S, it is not out of the question that, in the future, the price will once again attack its all-time highs — which it has finally reached.

Who would have thought that this bearish stock could return to its highs after losing 99%? Incredible, isn't it?

Case 8: Carvana (Solution)

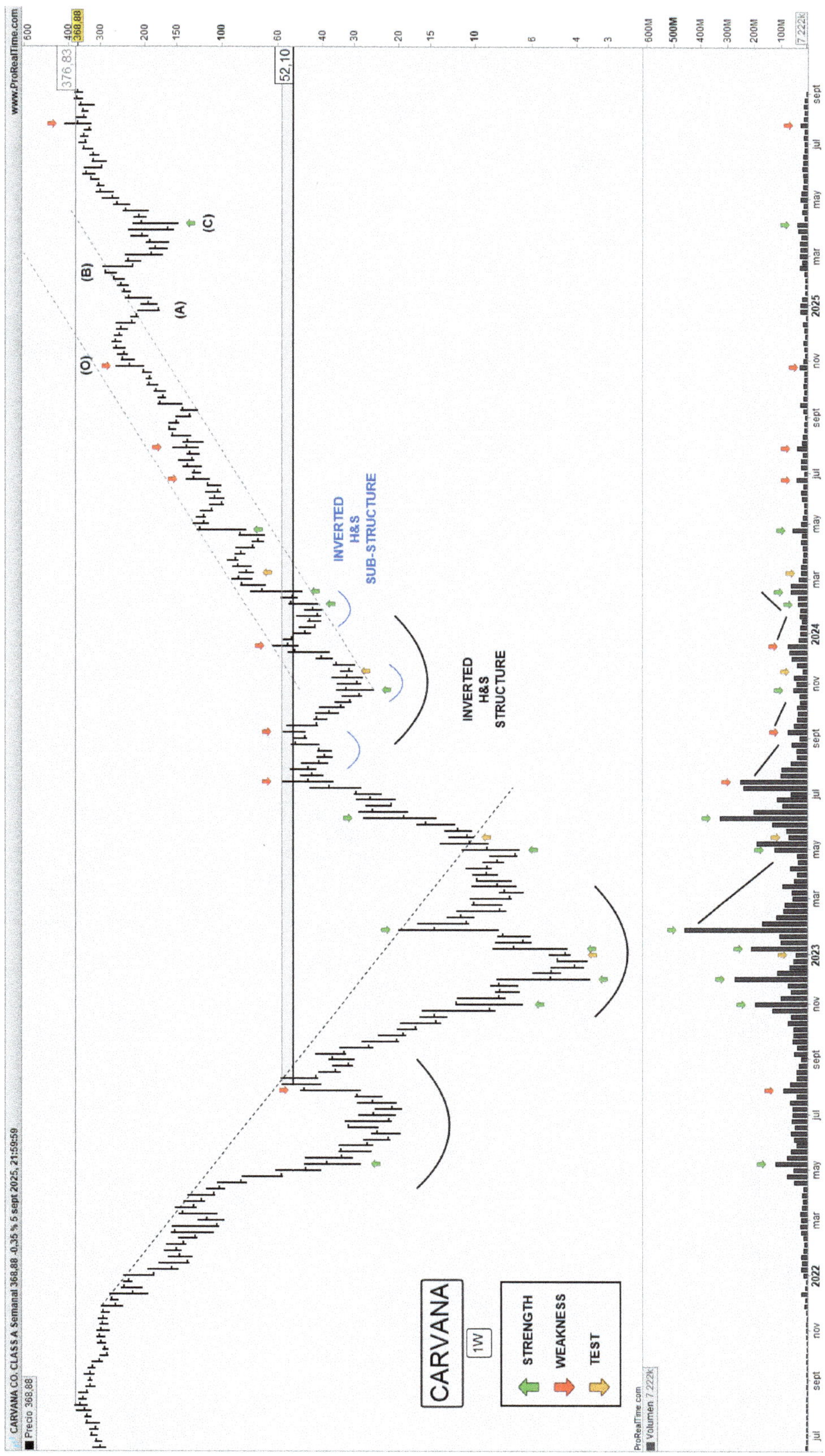

Case 9: Microstrategy

Now I present to you one of my favourite assets for 2024 and surely for 2025: Microstrategy.

This company, led by Michael Saylor, is closely related to the world of Bitcoin, given that its strategy has been to buy and accumulate this type of asset.

Leaving all this aside, the weekly chart has a lot of VSA reading.

The price comes from an impeccable uptrend on the left side of the chart, driven by the 2020 Bitcoin halving bull run.

However, supply was lurking in the $100 zone, where a very powerful BC occurs. Since then, the price has remained within a horizontal structure.

In an attempt to rebel, the value tried to approach the BC close, without success, producing an LPSY as Phase C. Immediately afterwards, the price broke downwards and, after testing the break, plummeted.

In that downward impulse, demand came back in to stop the price in the $15 zone, with a pronounced SC. Once again, a horizontal structure formed, which was able to break the downward trend line of the impulse. The drying up of supply was evident, and the value was finally able to break through the upper part. After testing it, it began its upward journey until it reached the resistance zone of $100, which it surpassed and consolidated above.

In Elliott's jargon, this consolidation formed a flat ABC corrective pattern with a C failure.

We will analyse this structure on the right in more detail in the next case study.

This is one of the maxims of VSA. We are looking at this chart on a weekly timeframe, and if we want to obtain more details of the professional footprint, we must lower the timeframes to detect possible clues left by the strong hands. From more to less.

To analyse the structure on the right in greater detail, we will move down to the daily chart and examine the characteristics of the formation that unfolded over several weeks.

Case 9: Microstrategy (Solution)

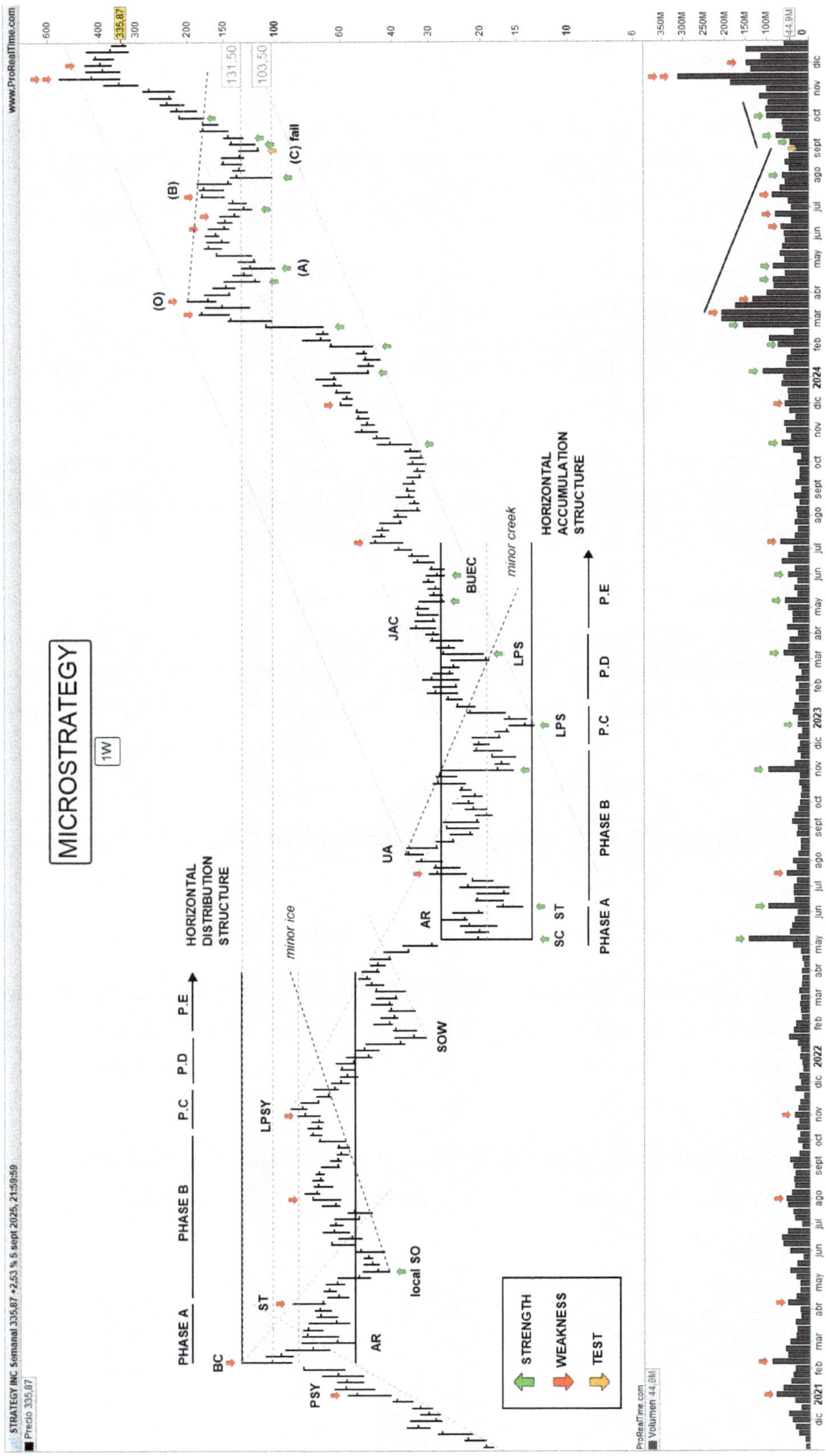

Case 10: Microstrategy

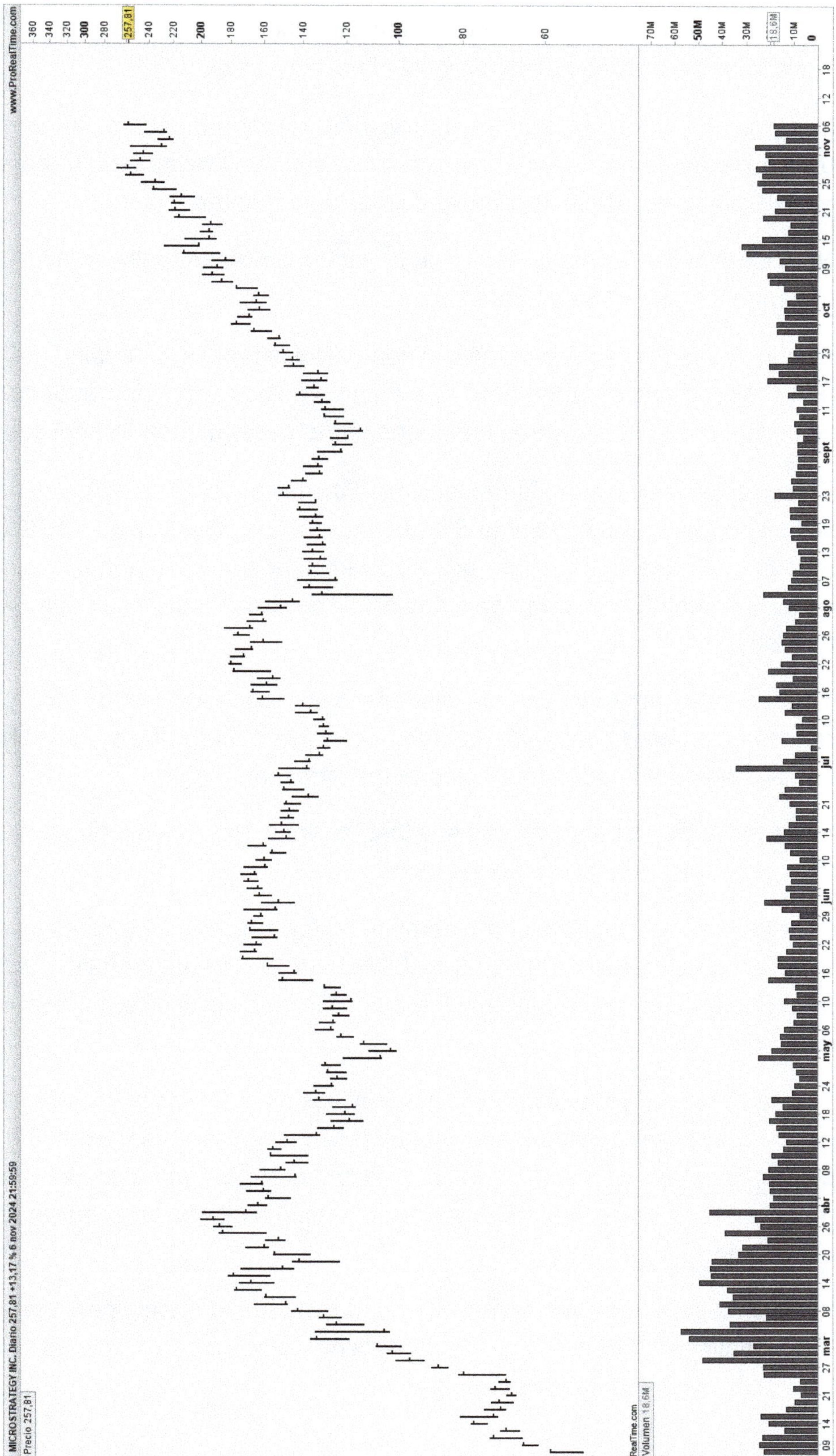

Let me show you the latest structure that Microstrategy was developing in the chart from the previous case, only now in a daily chart.

In it, we can see a large amount of volume on the left side of the chart, in bullish bars with hardly any displacement. Supply was present in the stock, showing that the bullish impulse had its days numbered.

No sooner said than done. The price broke the upward impulse trend line and began to develop a horizontal structure.

During Phase B, the price made two bearish false breaks, extending the lower part of the structure in the form of a local SO. After two failed attempts, the stock launched itself towards the upper part of the structure, without success.

This was followed by another extension of the lower part, this time much more violent and with greater volume. This event could be classified as a TSO within a Wyckoff Phase C. The price returned within the structure and as was to be expected, tested the lower part again to check the state of supply. And it worked.

You can see how the volume decreases throughout the structure until it reaches its lowest point with the TSO Test. From there, the price broke the minor creek and headed for the top of the structure.

In the most recent bars, you can see that the value has managed to overcome the major creek and is testing the break.

If we look at the complete chart, demand is now present, as evidenced by an increase in volume since the TSO test. 'Richard likes to see increasing volume from Phase C onwards,' says my mentor. All it needs to do is break definitively upwards.

If we also return to the chart from the previous case, which is the same asset but on a weekly timeframe, we can see how this entire structure on the daily chart occurs above the $100 resistance zone, suggesting that demand has managed to conquer that level and is absorbing all the supply that remained in that zone.

You can tell me what the final outcome of this structure was, now that it has been confirmed, but it has all the ingredients to continue its upward trend in the short, medium and long term.

Case 10: Microstrategy (Solution)

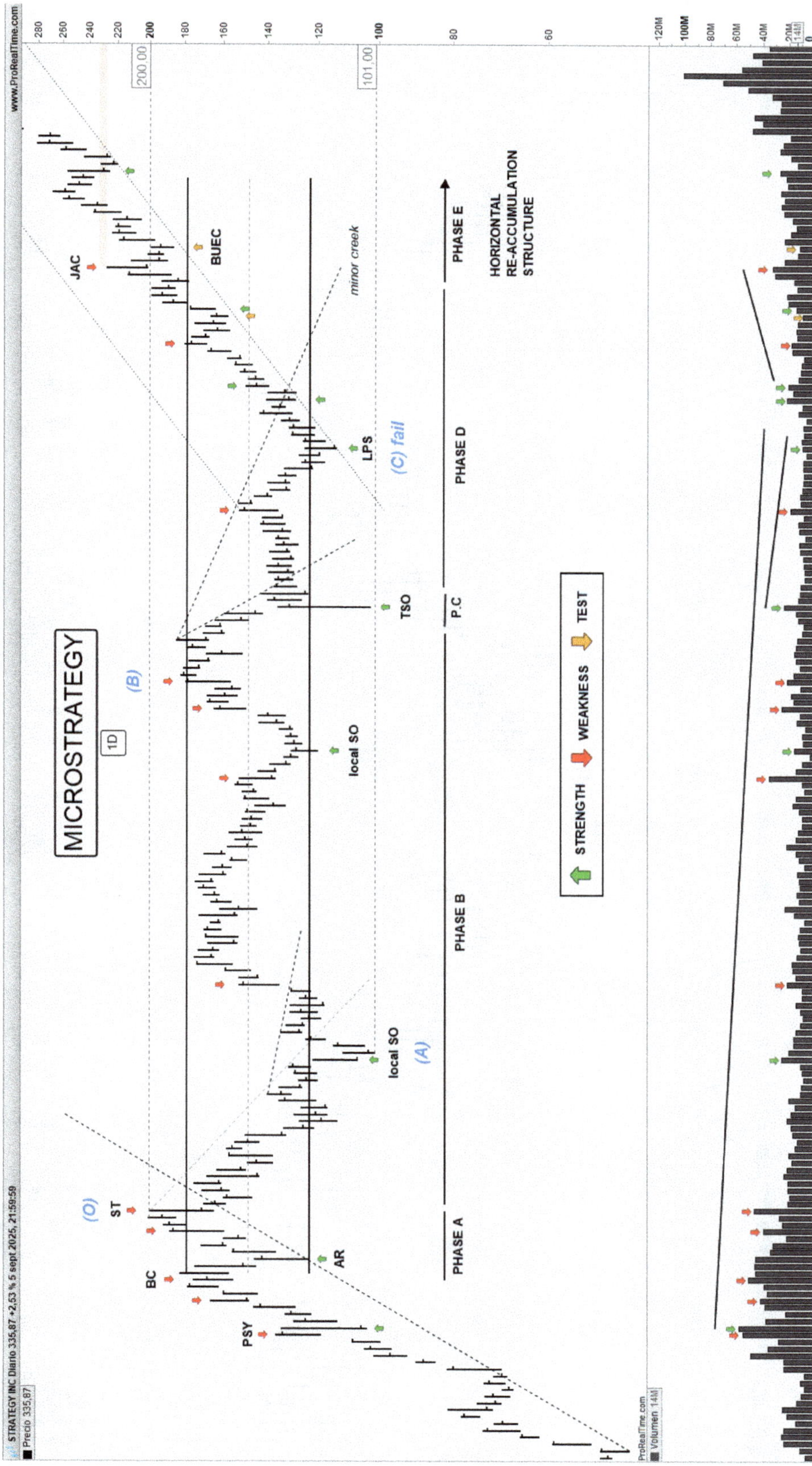

Case 11: NVIDIA

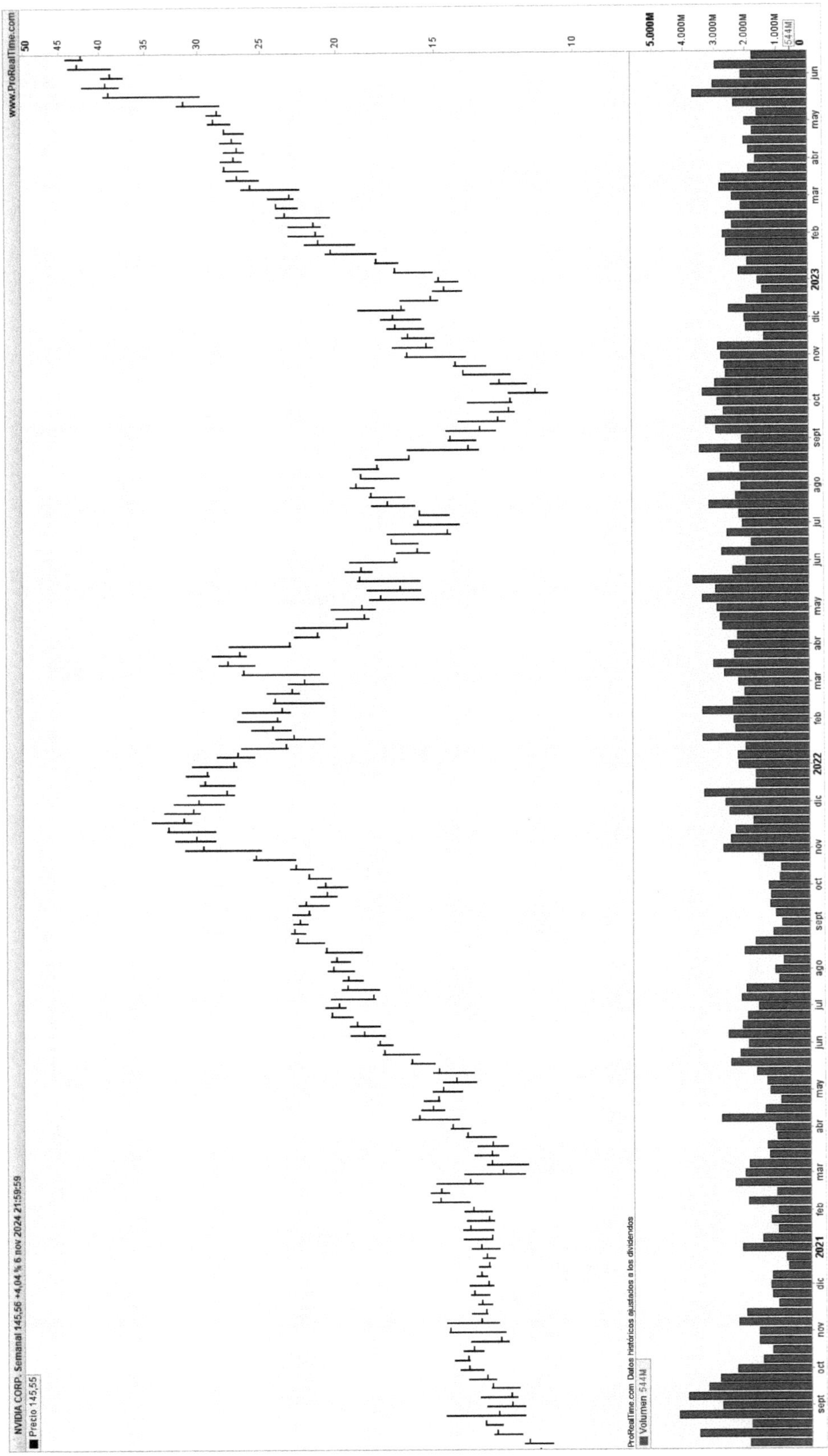

Let's now focus on the star asset of 2024: NVIDIA.

Amidst the stock market explosion in assets related to Artificial Intelligence, or AI for short, we find the most talked-about stock in recent months. But let's focus on the months leading up to the stock's big rise, from $10 to $140 in just over a year.

2021 and 2022, before the AI boom. The price had been on an upward trend for some time, until supply stopped the price in the $15 range. There, a triangular structure formed, drying up all supply in the market. After its particular TSO, the price broke through the top of the structure, tested it with a BUEC and accelerated its upward impulse. A stop along the way.

However, supply was lurking and entered the $30 zone, forming an abominable H&S weekly chart structure. After breaking the neckline with force, the price fell sharply.

However, it can be seen that the volume in many bearish bars was high until it reached the bottom of the triangular re-accumulation structure again, which served as support.

However, in an attempt to break that level, the value made a bearish bar, with a relatively narrow range, climatic volume and in a new zone. The following week, the price reversed strongly, leaving connotations of the previous bag holding bar. In fact, that bar caused a V-shaped return to the $18 resistance zone.

In the subsequent pullback, supply withdrew, and an inverted H&S formed. The break of the neckline and the downward trend line, almost in a coinciding price zone, initiated the subsequent bull run of Artificial Intelligence.

However, before moving from $15 to $140, the professional carried out all these manoeuvres to accumulate as many shares as possible in an area that they considered attractive at the time.

It is also not very common to see a H&S followed by an inverted H&S and given the impact that the stock has had during 2024, it was a chart that had to be included in the case studies in this book.

Case 11: NVIDIA (Solution)

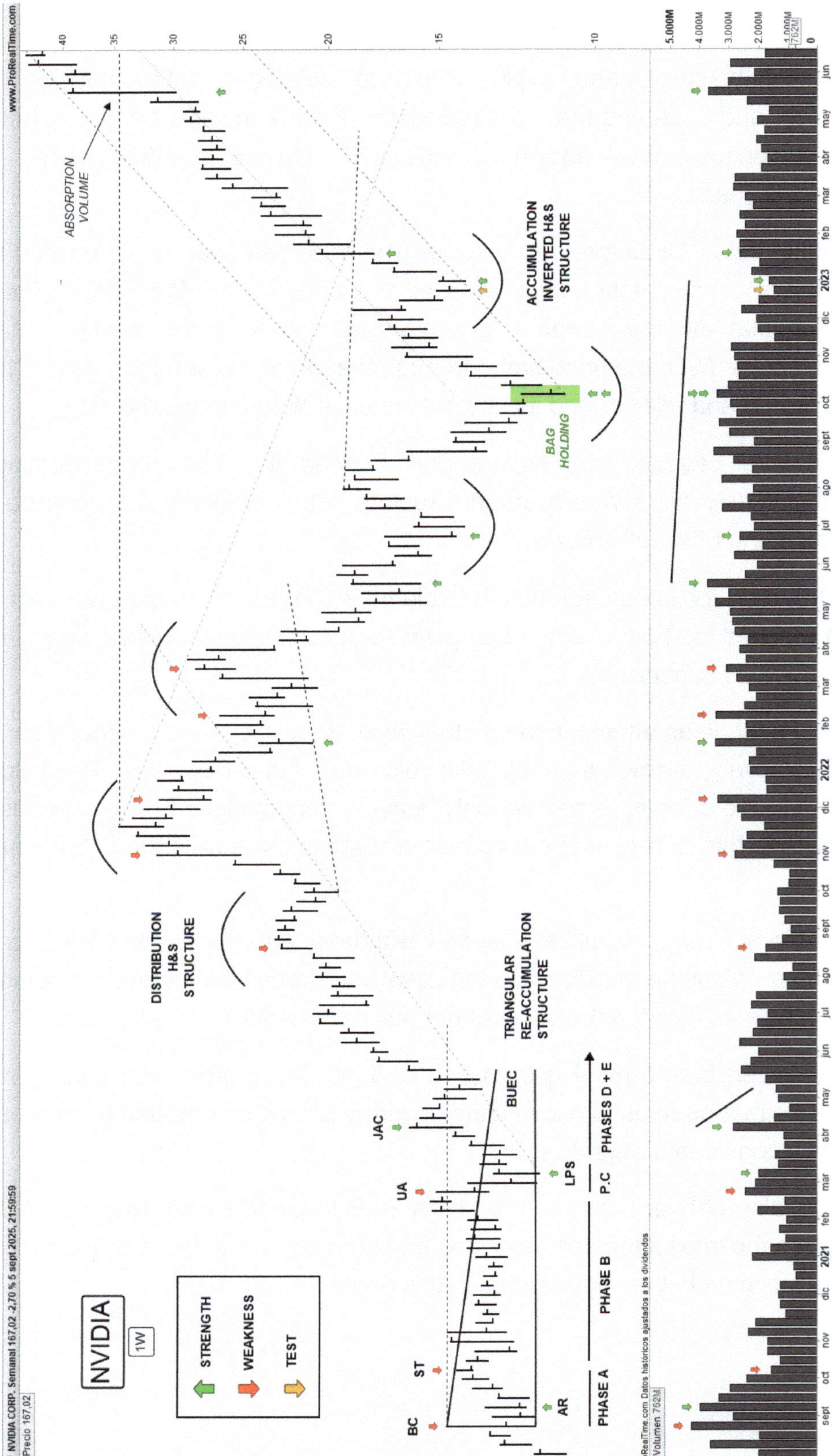

Case 12: PayPal

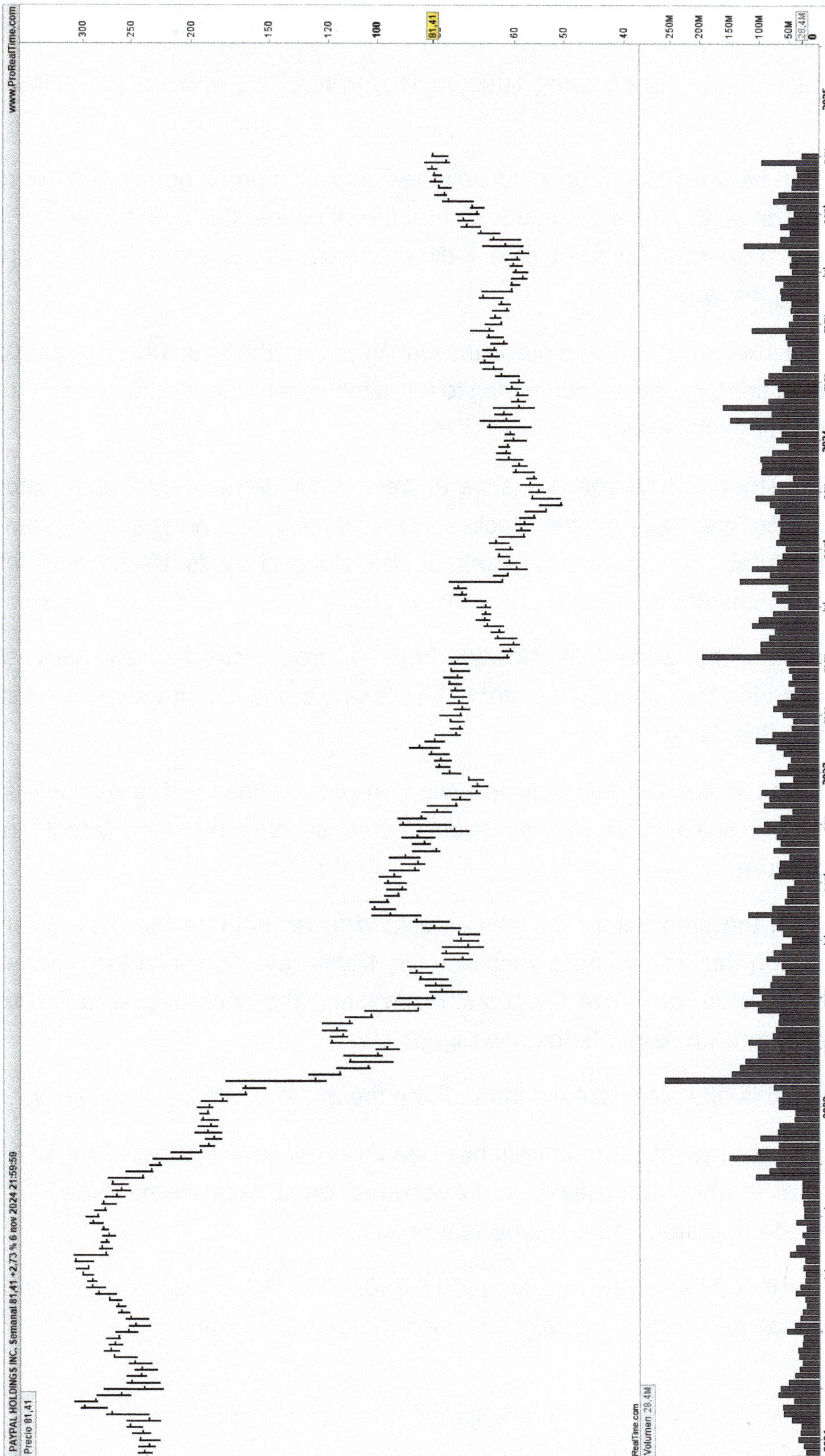

PayPal is an asset that enjoyed a long run of gains until it hit a rough patch.

The price had been rising spectacularly until 2021, which is when this case study begins.

It can be seen that supply entered the value for a prolonged period, forming a horizontal structure. So much so that the price lost the bullish channel it had been respecting for some time, indicating that this was more than just a pause along the way.

After several attempts to break through the top of the structure, the price broke down sharply. Before continuing to fall, it tested whether demand was present, with a negative result.

The stock fell sharply for several bars, until demand gradually returned, slowing the pace of the decline. This is very characteristic of triangular structures. Supply is too strong to be stopped in its tracks and form a horizontal structure.

Instead, the price falls slowly, drop by drop, with demand very slowly absorbing the supply in the stock. This is why triangular structures are formed, as in this case.

The price was trapped between two non-parallel lines with a negative slope. Volume spikes can also be seen in bearish bars near the bottom of the structure.

When the time came, the stock decided to accentuate the falls and broke through this line, without success. The bar is reversed, and the minimum of the structure or Phase C occurs. From there, the price begins to restructure itself, making higher highs and higher lows.

With this, the stock breaks through the top of the structure and tests it.

The subsequent development has been a consolidation around the $67 level, the area where the selling climax occurred, and it now seems to be forming a long-term bottom in the shape of a mushroom.

Note that these round numbers (100, 200, 300...) mark psychological levels of support and resistance. Will this happen again this time?

Case 12: PayPal (Solution)

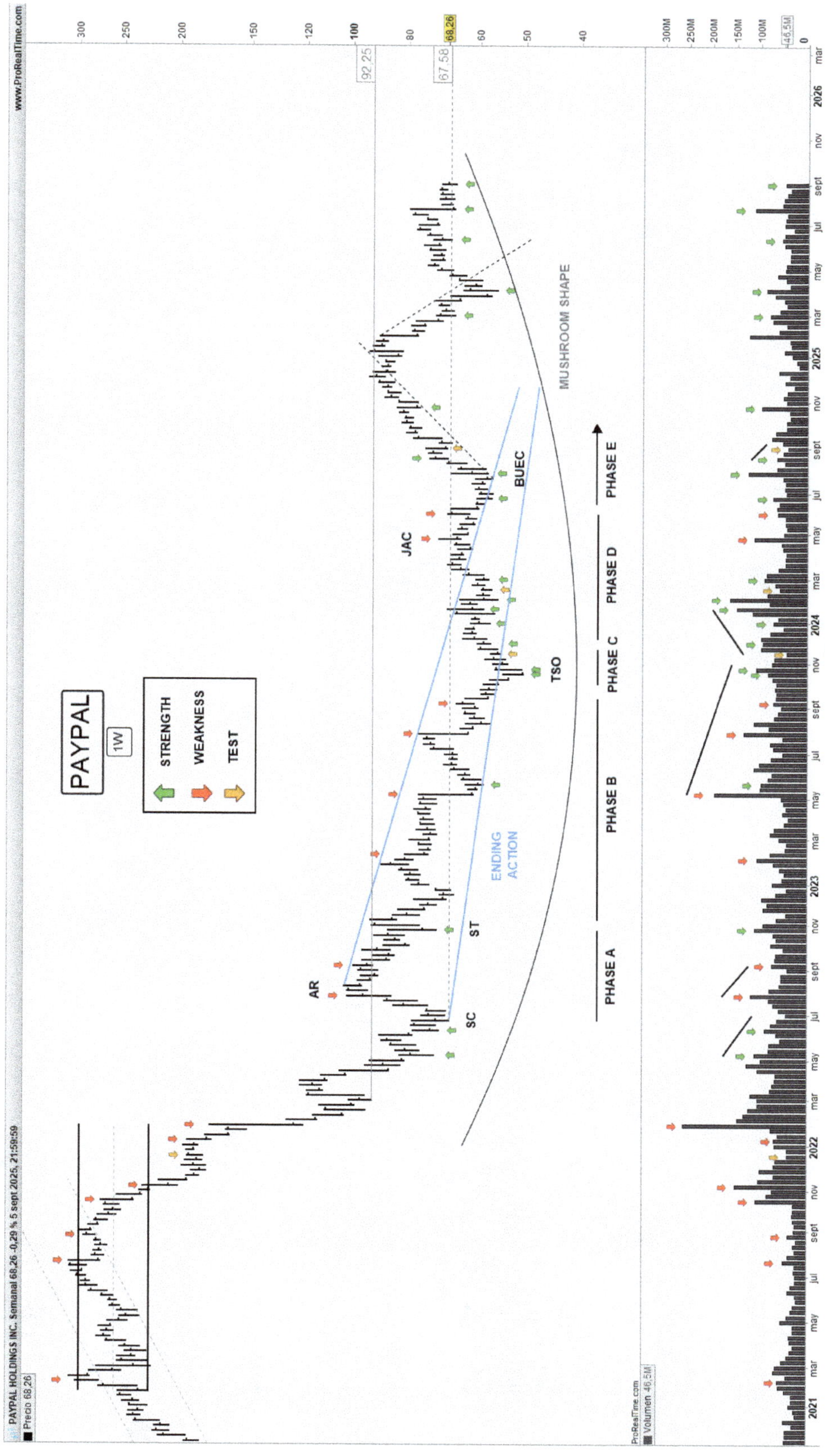

Case 13: Palantir

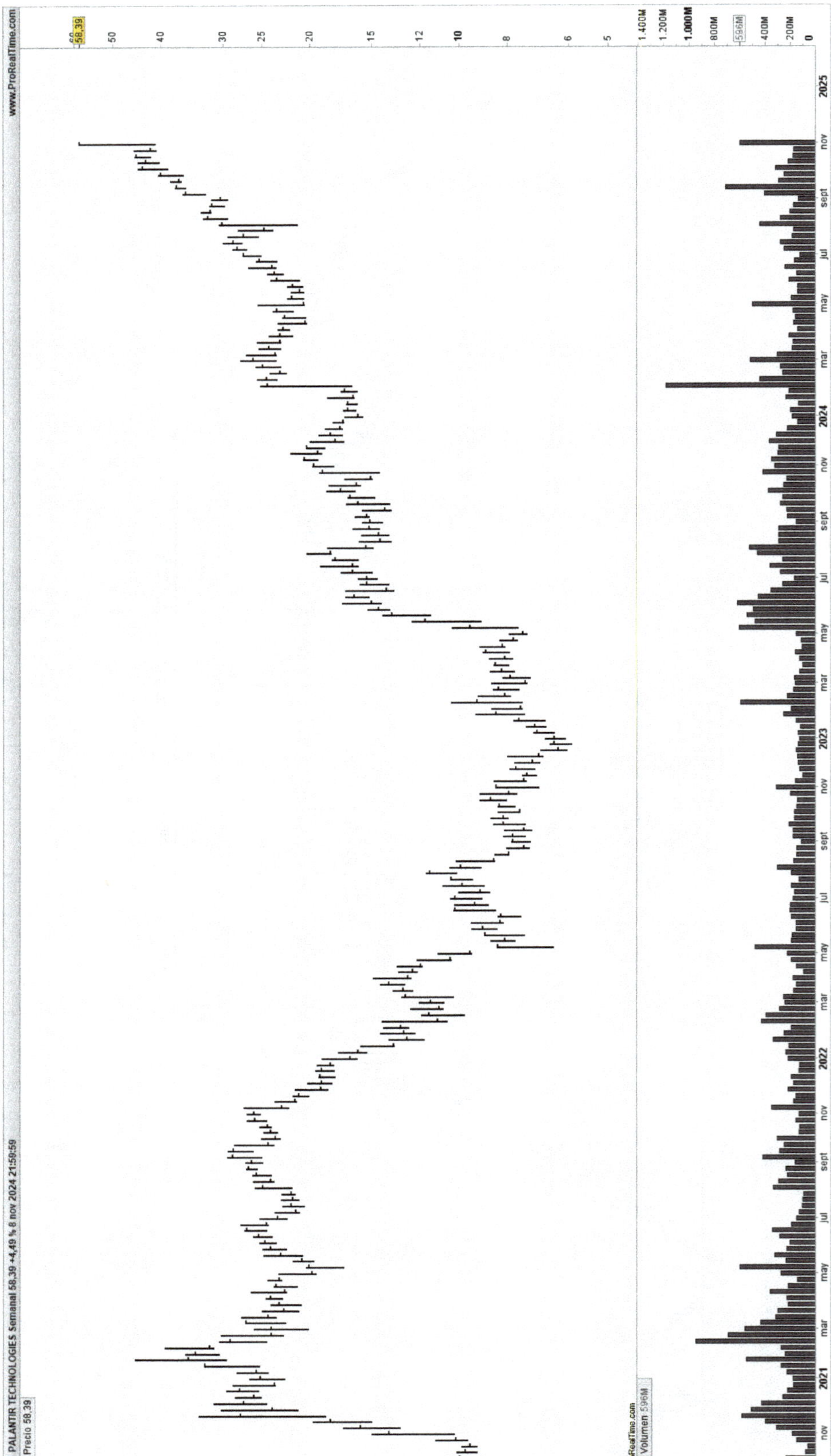

Let us now focus on another stock that recently went public.

In fact, its performance is very similar to that of other IPOs in the US market: it goes public, there is an upward impulse that traps investors, the price plummets, then moves sideways and begins a sustained upward trend, exceeding IPO levels.

In the case of Palantir, these market phases occurred with great precision.

The price began trading and experienced a strong upward impulse, until supply entered the asset like a bull. From there, large volume spikes were seen in bullish bars, and a horizontal structure began to form. When the strong hands detected that there was no more demand in the market, the price broke down sharply, initiating a large bearish impulse that broke the levels at which the stock began trading.

When the time came, the price slowed down, motivated by the entry of demand into the equation. This produced another horizontal structure, which was able to reverse the situation and give rise to an upward impulse, breaking the long-term downward trend line.

This movement was supported by large amounts of volume backing the upward movement.

Supply came in to stop the price again, creating another base or horizontal structure, which again resolved upwards. Subsequently, supply reappeared and a new horizontal structure formed. After a violent movement in Phase C, the stock also resolved upwards, allowing the rises to continue.

The impulse was structured within an upward channel at all times.

At present, the stock has already broken historical highs. All of this was driven by a long process of accumulation, intermediate re-accumulation structures and their respective upward impulse.

Case 13: Palantir (Solution)

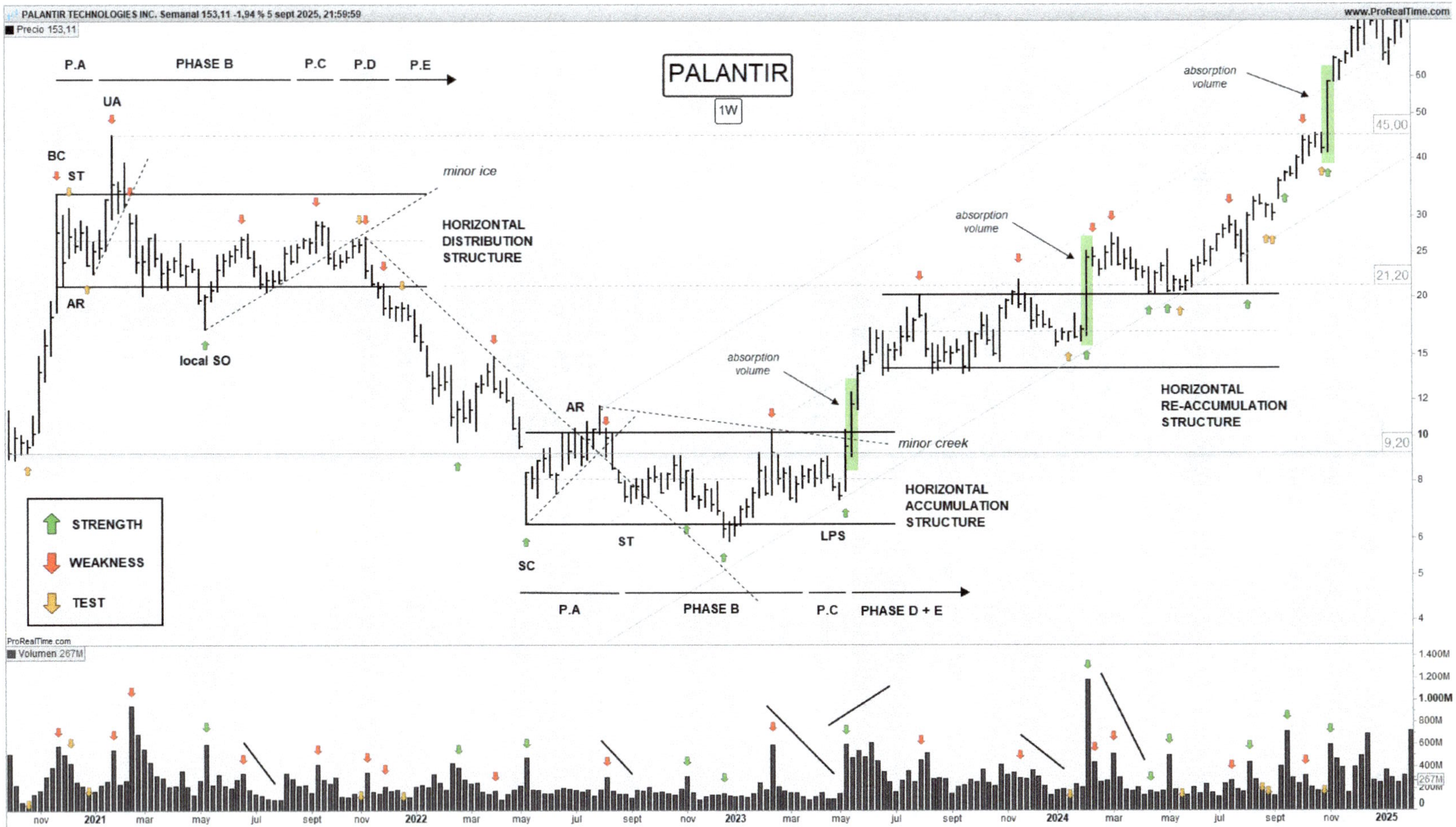

Case 14: Block

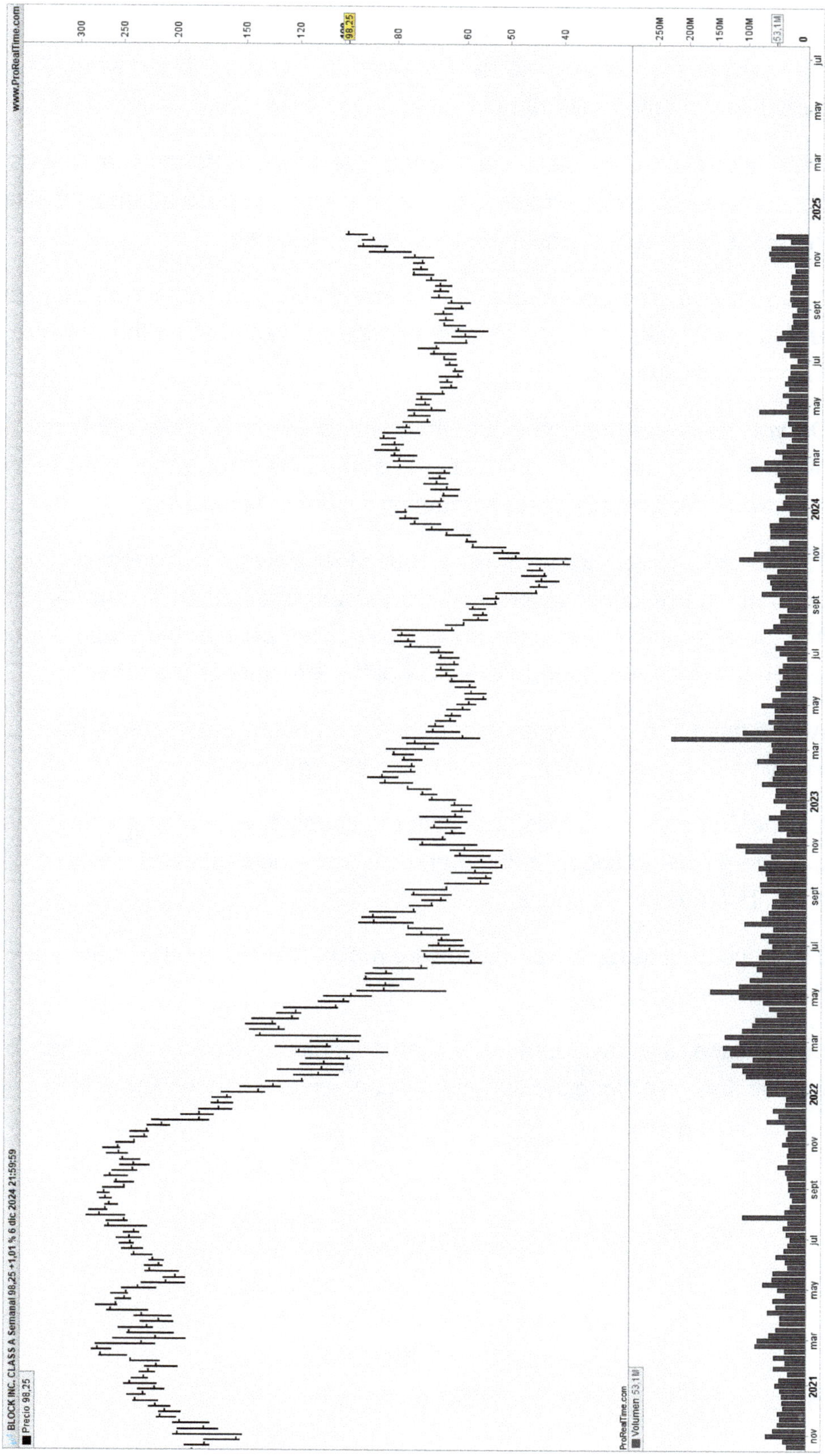

Let's look at another case study, this time a little more complicated to analyse than the ones we've seen so far. Perhaps you noticed this too when you were "scribbling" on the chart, right?

Let's take it step by step. On the left, the value is forming a well-defined horizontal structure. In Phase C of this structure, the price attempts to rise, but the bar is reversed, so the intentions were not to rise.

And so it was. The price broke downwards with a gotcha bar and successfully tested the break. The path of least resistance was now on the downside, so the value fell sharply.

Do you remember the previous chart where demand could not immediately overcome supply, but gradually absorbed it throughout the triangular structure? Well, in this case, something similar is happening.

The chart shows volume spikes that slow down the speed of the price declines, but it continues to fall. During this process, you can see that a horizontal structure with a downward bias (even an inverted H&S) is forming, where the price moves from one side of the structure to the other.

At one point, the price expands the lower part but re-enters the structure. How many times have I written this sentence already, right?

On the first attempt, it fails and tests the supply level. Once it was confirmed that there was no supply in the market, it broke upwards and attacked the AR zone, but massive supply appeared.

The price then made a new downward move, re-entering the structure, where demand emerged again.

In this case, the development of the horizontal structure with a bearish bias was evident, but along the way supply came in and prices were tested at lower levels once more.

Case 14: Block (Solution)

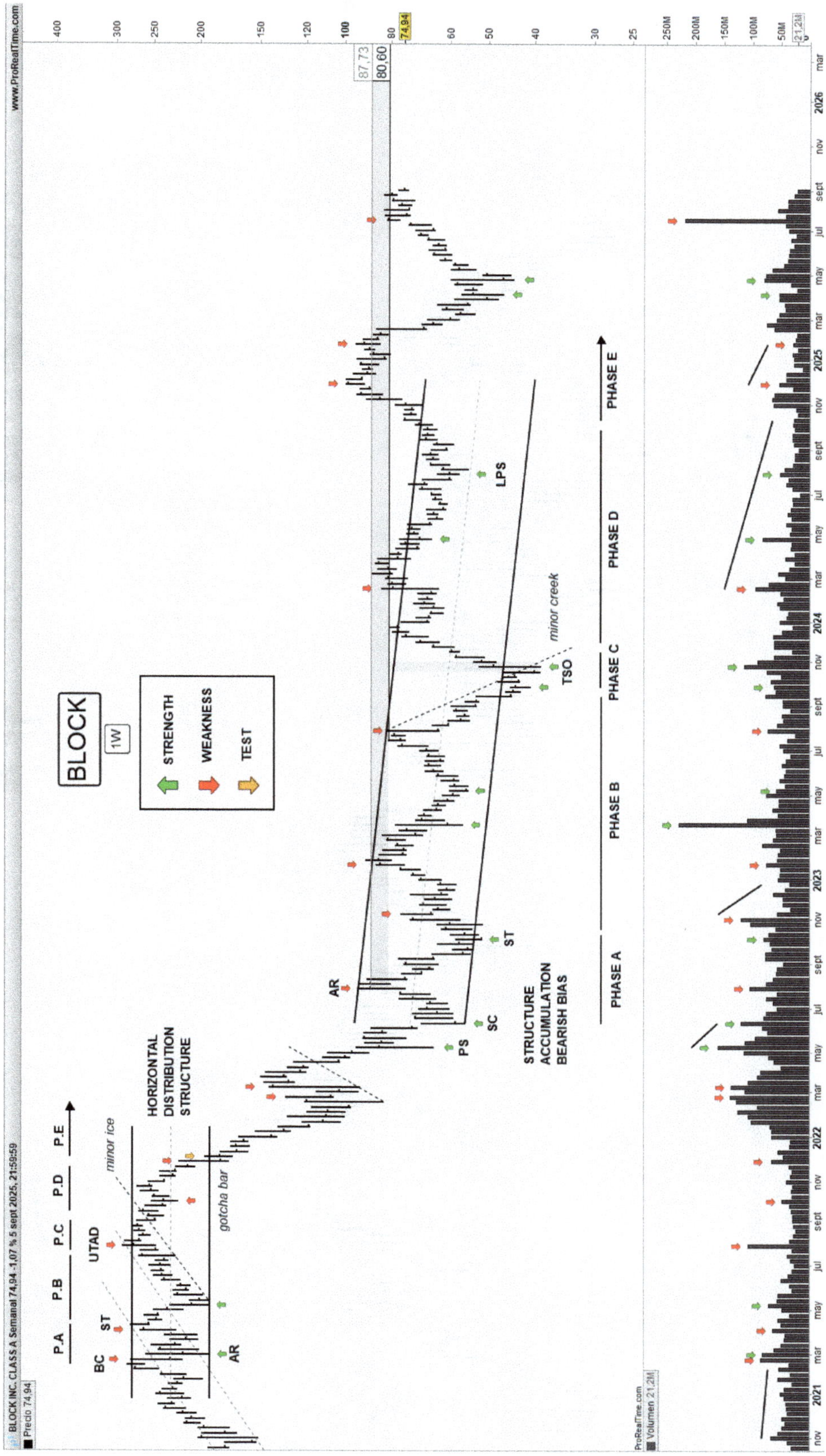

Case 15: Bitcoin miners ETF

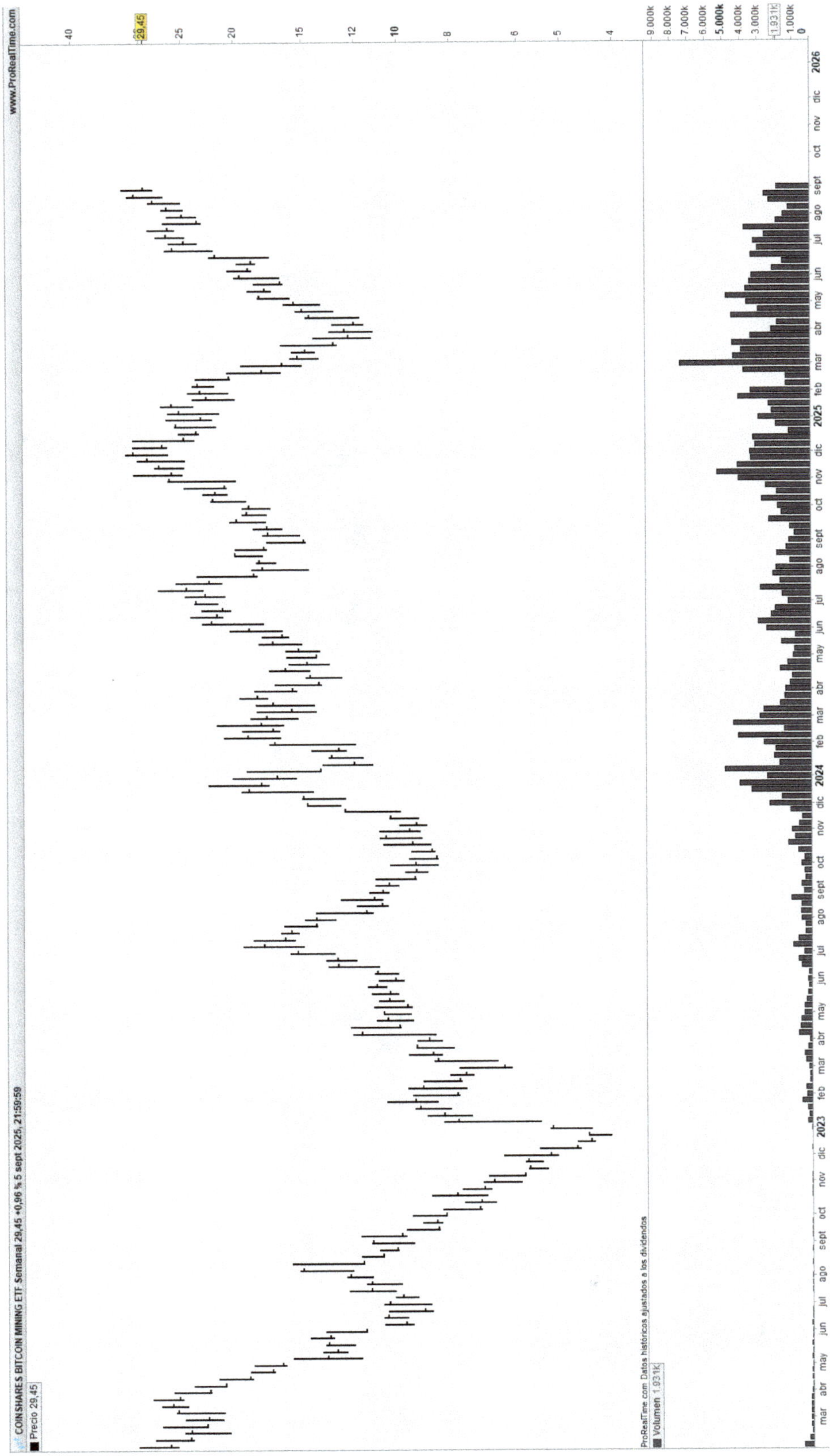

Stocks, cryptocurrencies, commodities, and now ETFs! This methodology can be used to analyse any listed, liquid asset that is subject to the law of supply and demand, as you can see.

In this case, the ETF (or exchange-traded fund) represents the main Bitcoin mining companies, on a weekly chart.

Since it was listed, the fall could not have been steeper and more relentless. All the impulse was well defined within a bearish channel.

At one point, it reached the bottom of the channel and the price managed to react and break through the top of it. Later, it successfully tested the broken bearish channel. This started an upward impulse that is targeting the next lower highs in the $15 area.

In that area, the price rose above the key level and then fell back below it, initiating another downward impulse. However, it can be seen that the volume does not accompany the price, creating a divergence in volume and indicating that professionals are not willing to see lower prices. So much so that the price breaks the downward trend line and another upward trend begins.

At this point, it can be seen that the key $15 zone is the level to beat. The value is also performing an inverted H&S, which must be confirmed.

Later, the price breaks through the $15 level again and a structure begins to form around the neckline and key area of the inverted H&S. The lows are getting higher, and the highs are levelling off horizontally.

At a certain point, the price breaks downward and halts at the AR zone, showing strength. The price broke through the minor creek, the upper part of the structure, and is now preparing to assault new highs. Will it succeed?

Case 15: Bitcoin miners ETF (Solution)

Case 16: Cameco Corporation

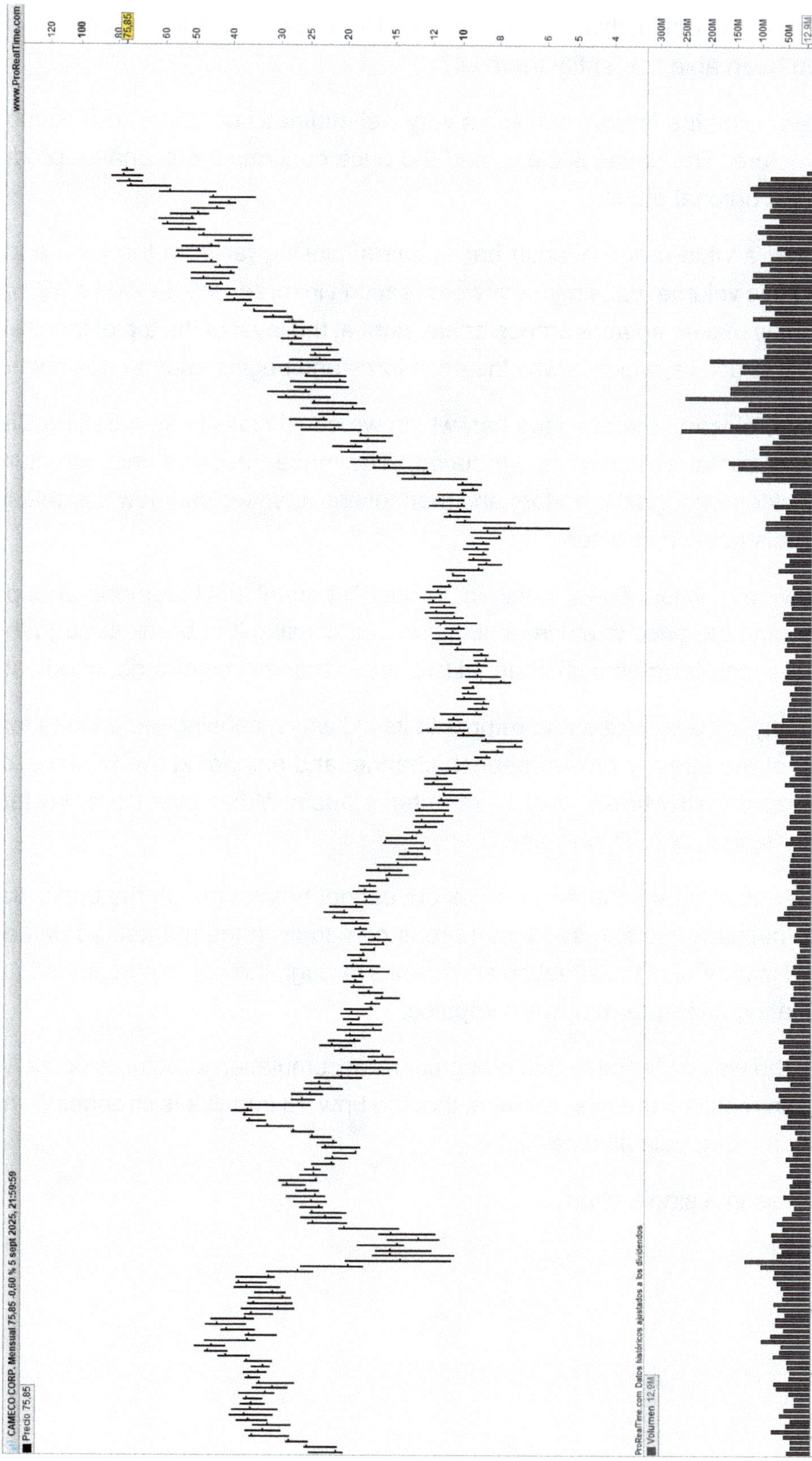

Let us now look at this case study with at least four structures to analyse. Have you been able to identify them all?

Starting on the left, we can see a very well-defined horizontal H&S distribution structure. The cause is clear, and the price confirms the scenario, producing a proportional effect.

Later, a wide-range bearish bar appears, closing far from the lows and with climatic volume, causing an upward reaction in three well-defined ABC waves. Supply makes an appearance again, right at the level of the top of the previous H&S structure, which is why the price turns and begins another downward leg.

At the close of the previous bar, which we could classify as a Selling Climax, a horizontal structure is produced. The price resolves this structure by breaking through the bottom and then testing it, so we can now say that it was a redistribution structure.

Now, the value flows within a bearish channel until demand reappears, bringing the price to a screeching halt and causing it to break through the top of the long-term bearish channel (we are in monthly timeframe, mind you).

Supply is not satisfied and returns to its old ways, causing the price to test the top of the already broken bearish channel and extending the SC level of the horizontal structure... only to re-enter it again. What event are we facing? That's right, a TSO in Phase C.

The value breaks the minor creek but cannot break through the upper part. In the pullback, we can see that there is no supply in the market, so demand is now in control of the situation and breaks through the upper part, subsequently initiating a long-term upward impulse.

On the way up, another two triangular re-accumulation structures occur, which again resolves the rise, showing that the upward impulse is stronger than ever and making new all-time-highs.

All this in a single chart.

Case 16: Cameco Corporation (Solution)

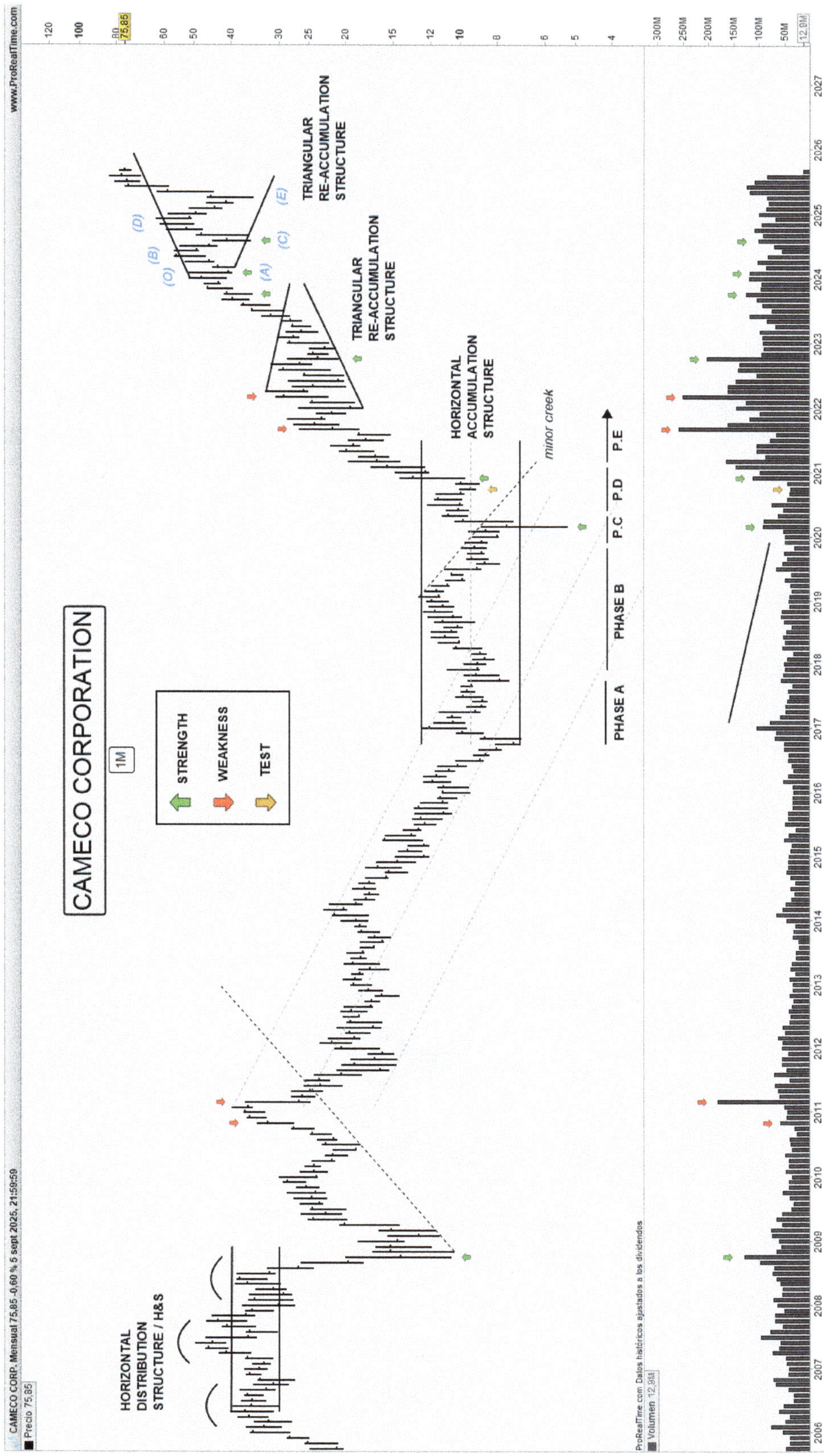

Case 17: Crowdstrike

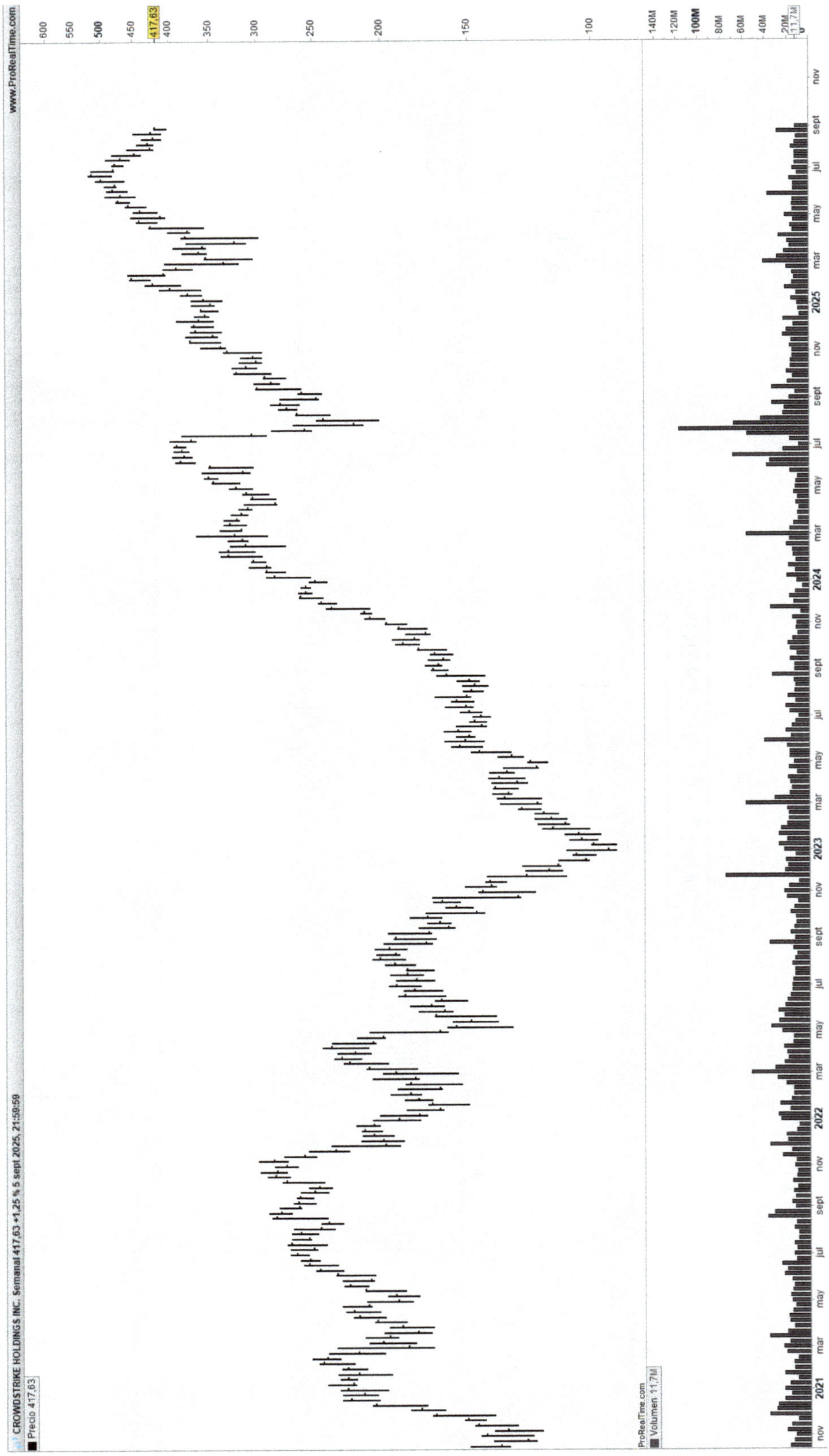

Perhaps you've heard of this cybersecurity company, right? In the summer of 2024, during peak vacation season, there was a global computer outage caused by a failed software update from Crowdstrike on Microsoft's servers. Hundreds of flights were cancelled, and many personal and business computers didn't function normally that day.

This led to an unprecedented drop in the stock's value, as can be seen on the right side of the chart. But could this have been anticipated? Let's analyze the chart step by step.

On the left, you can clearly see a distribution structure in the form of a Head and Shoulders pattern (H&S). The neckline was in the $175 zone and was broken after several attempts. The subsequent downward impulse followed an expanding triangular structure, which is uncommon in the market. So much so that the five ABCDE waves can be perfectly distinguished.

The last of these, wave E, was unable to reach the bottom of the triangle, showing some weakness in the bearish impulse. Demand was entering the stock, which halted the declines and broke the top of the expanding triangle, initiating a bullish impulse.

This impulse was structured within a long-term bullish channel. If we look at Elliott Wave Theory, we can see five waves upward and a key peculiarity.

After breaking the $300 level, which coincided with the all-time highs and the head of the H&S on the left, the price made strange upward movements, driven by narrow-range bullish bars and ultra-climactic volumes, with gaps in between. All of this occurred after completing five upward waves. This should put us on high alert. If the price is able to absorb all that supply, great. If not, watch out.

Immediately after, the price broke lower, triggered by the software update incident, and the price broke the bullish channel. Could it have been predicted? I'll leave that to you.

After the violent break of the $300 level, a sharp V-shaped reversal occurred, leading to new all-time highs.

Case 17: Crowdstrike (Solution)

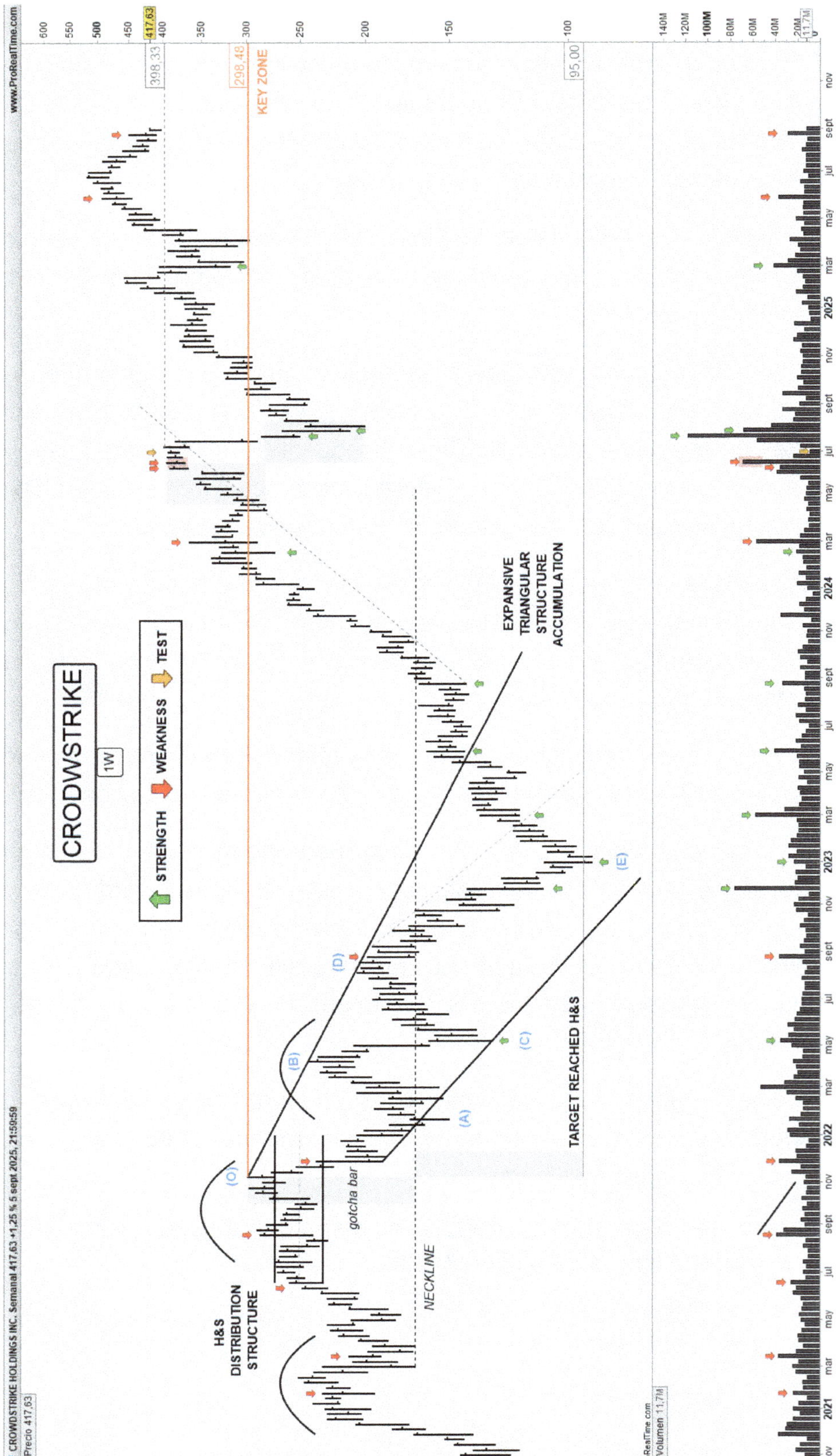

Case 18: Celsius Holdings

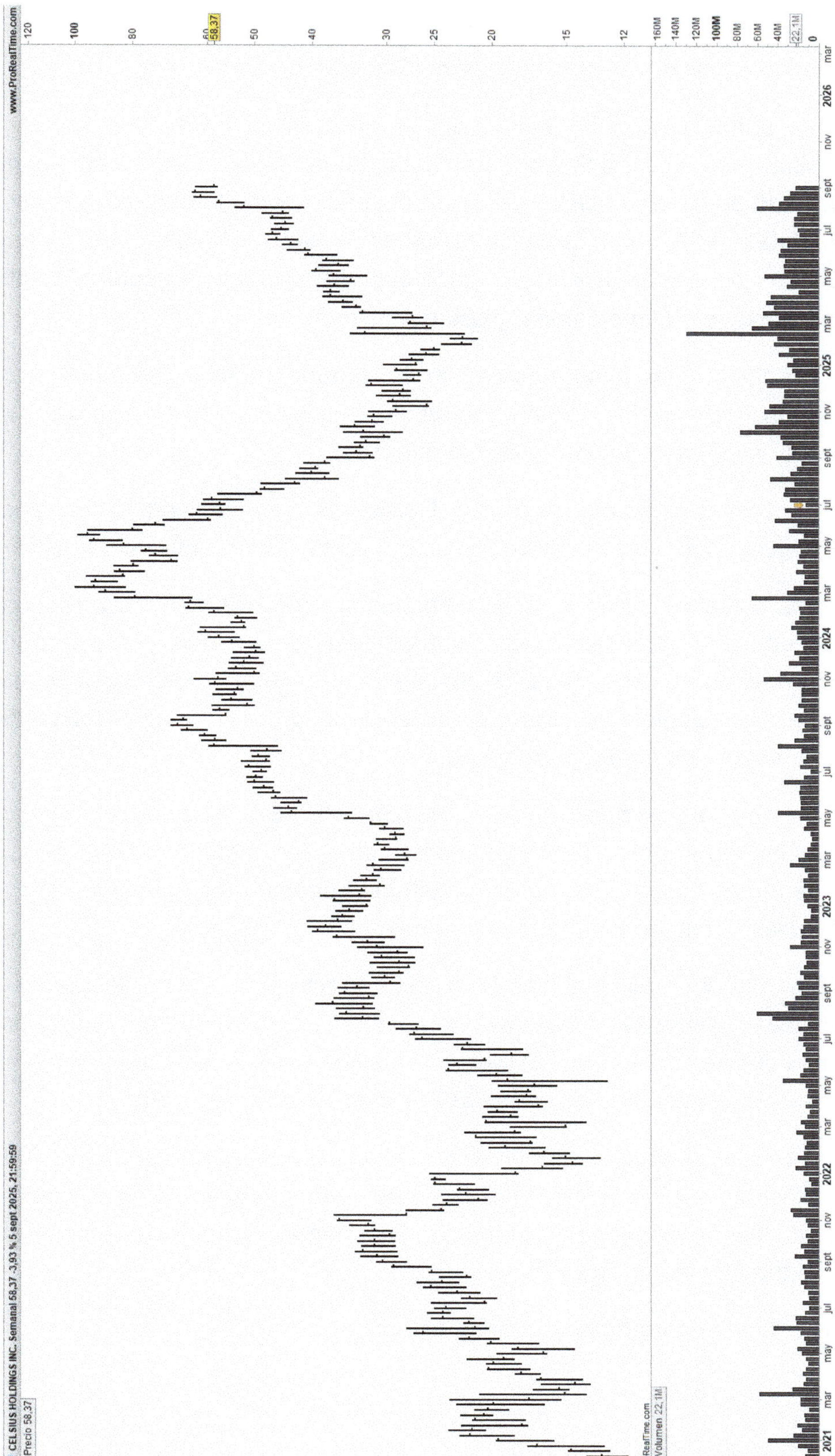

I have included this case study because during 2024, this stock was widely discussed on social media: Celsius Holdings.

One of the maxims I follow on social media when I see users posting their opinions about a stock is the psychology behind it all. When an asset rises a lot and starts an exponential upward trend, social media and certain news outlets are filled with fantastic comments about it. The same thing happens, but in reverse, when a stock's price plummets, with very negative comments and whispers of the company going bankrupt.

Faced with everything we hear on social media and in the news, we have charts. They are the only things that can truly tell us, in their own way, what is really happening with the asset in question.

The recent chaos surrounding Celsius is very striking. This American company had a very positive run on the stock market, until very recently.

If we look at the chart, numerous horizontal structures have occurred, both for accumulation and distribution, but with an upward bias. In fact, the stock followed an impeccable bullish channel for a long time. However, a point came when the volumes on bullish bars in new areas were very high, which indicated that supply was present in the stock.

This was exacerbated in the $100 zone (a psychological level). A model distribution structure occurred there, with a very short Phase A, as can be seen in the chart. That model distribution structure or double top led to the breakdown of the long-term bullish channel.

If the bullish impulse is long-term, the correction must be proportional to the impulse. Therefore, if we draw the Fibonacci levels of the entire impulse, we get three key zones. One of them is a confluence with the bottom of a previous re-accumulation structure, the 38.2% level, and the $28 zone.

Interestingly, that is the level the stock touched, and demand entered. Coincidence? Throughout the fall, there were voices saying it would soon stop, but the price doesn't stop in an intermediate zone; it stops in key zones, like the one we just mentioned.

The most important thing is price and price!

Case 18: Celsius Holdings (Solution)

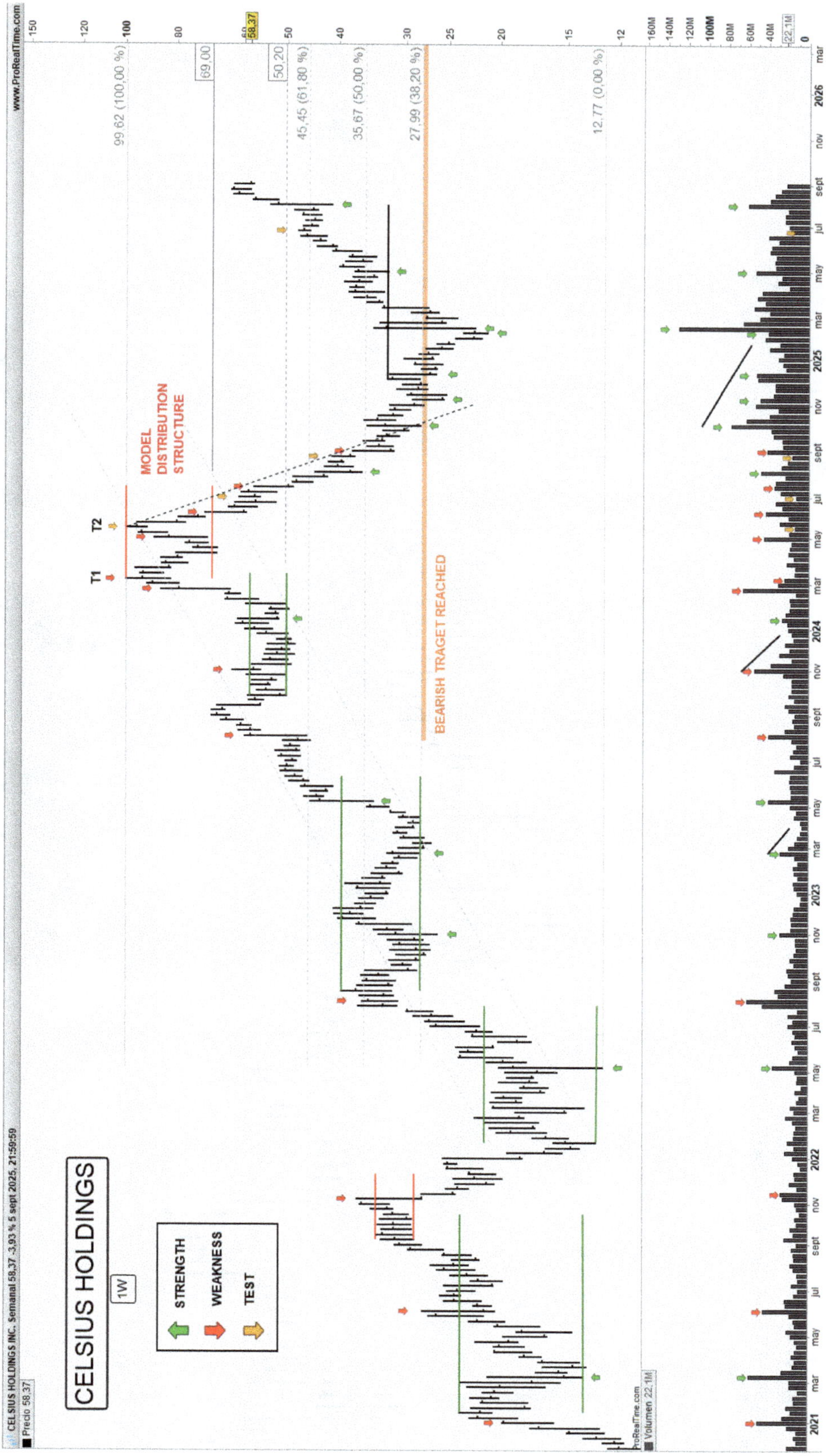

Case 19: Bitcoin / USD

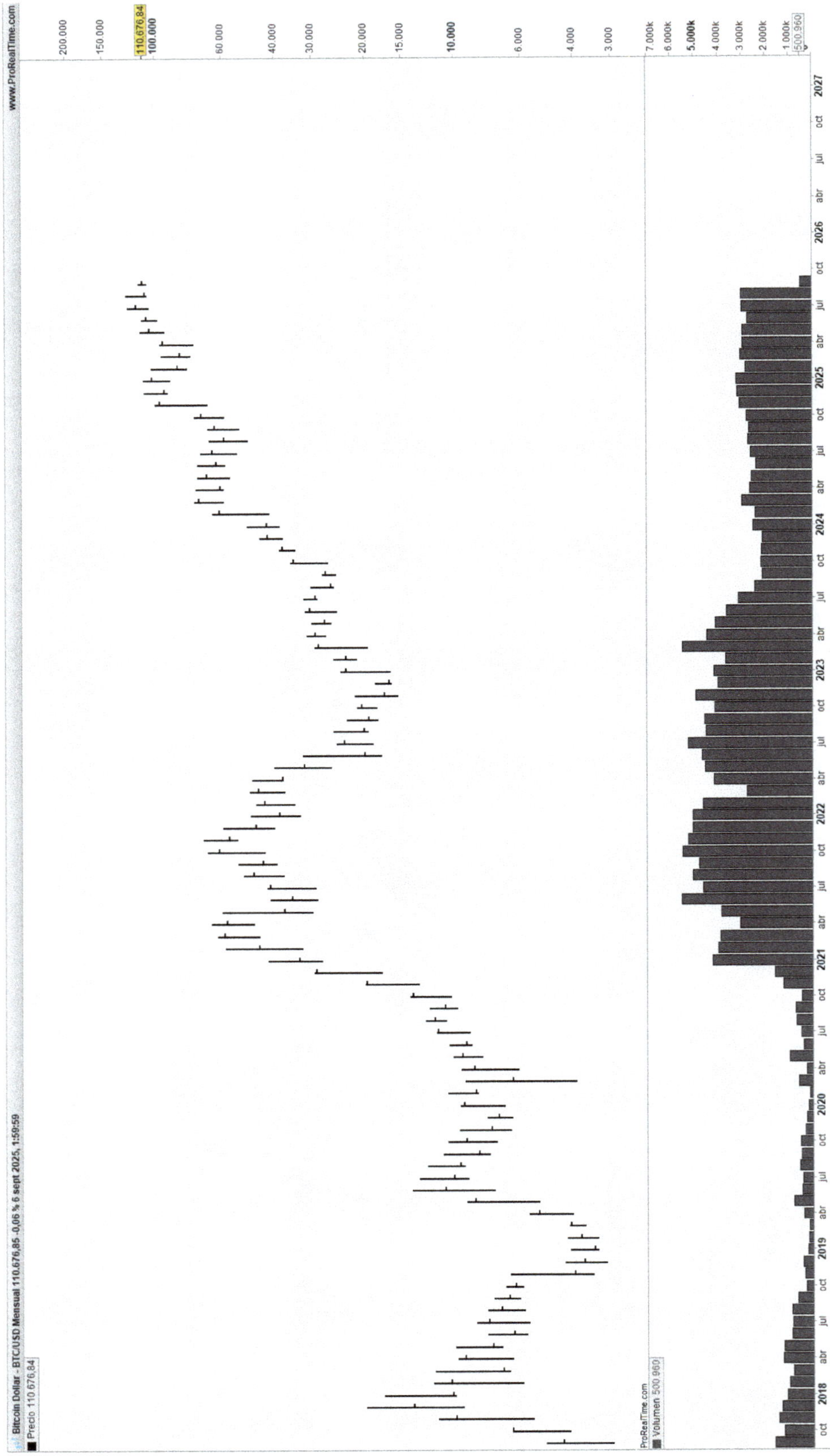

To finish off, I've put together two very long-term charts that perfectly illustrate the implications of the current movements for the two most talked-about assets in the world: Bitcoin and the S&P 500.

Let's start with Bitcoin. As you will have seen throughout the book, we've analysed a lot of charts for this asset, on daily, weekly, and now monthly scales. Do I like this asset?

It's crucial to point out that the logarithmic scale highlights how important it is to use this type of scale in charts. If you were to try and analyse Bitcoin's monthly chart on a linear scale, you wouldn't be able to see much of its history with any clarity.

Since 2018, the price has shown a series of remarkable movements that clearly reflect the dynamics between supply and demand. Practically during the 2018–2020 period, the market entered a corrective phase, unfolding in the form of an ABC pattern with a failed C-wave.

This failure acted as a powerful signal of strength, triggering an explosive upward move that carried the price to new all-time highs in the $60,000 region.

From that peak, the market established a major top, which eventually led to a sharp retracement back toward the previous all-time highs set in 2018. When the price reached that critical level, demand reappeared with strong conviction, sparking another upward movement.

This rally has been guided by a well-defined bullish trendline, which, interestingly, still remains intact today and continues to provide support for the long-term uptrend.

What stands out even more is a recurring pattern observed in monthly charts: every major market top so far has been formed by a very specific two-bar configuration—commonly referred to as a “top reversal.”

This raises the question that always appears at the edge of new highs and possible turning points: will this time be any different, or will history repeat itself once again?

Case 19: Bitcoin / USD (Solution)

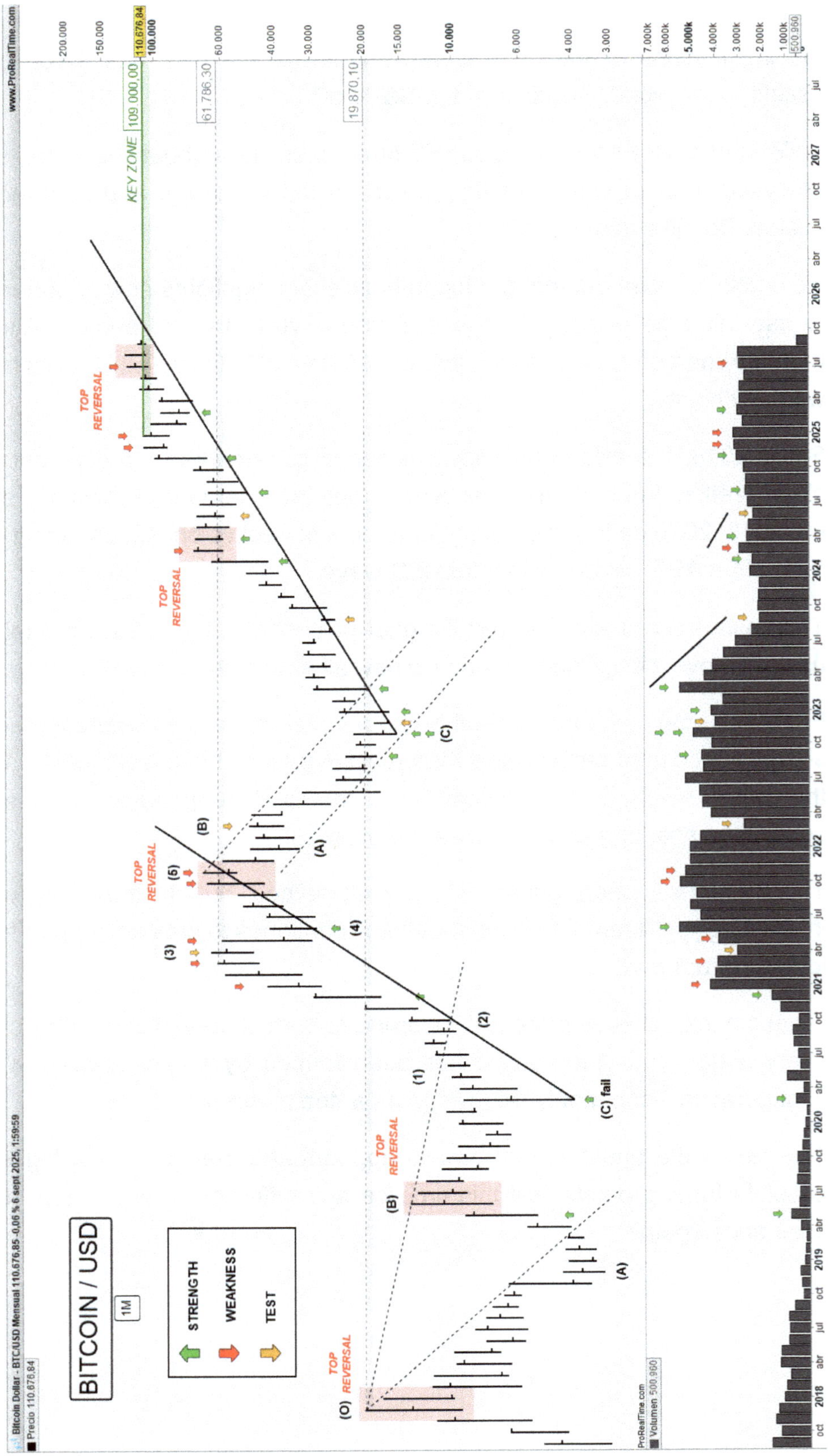

Case 20: SP500

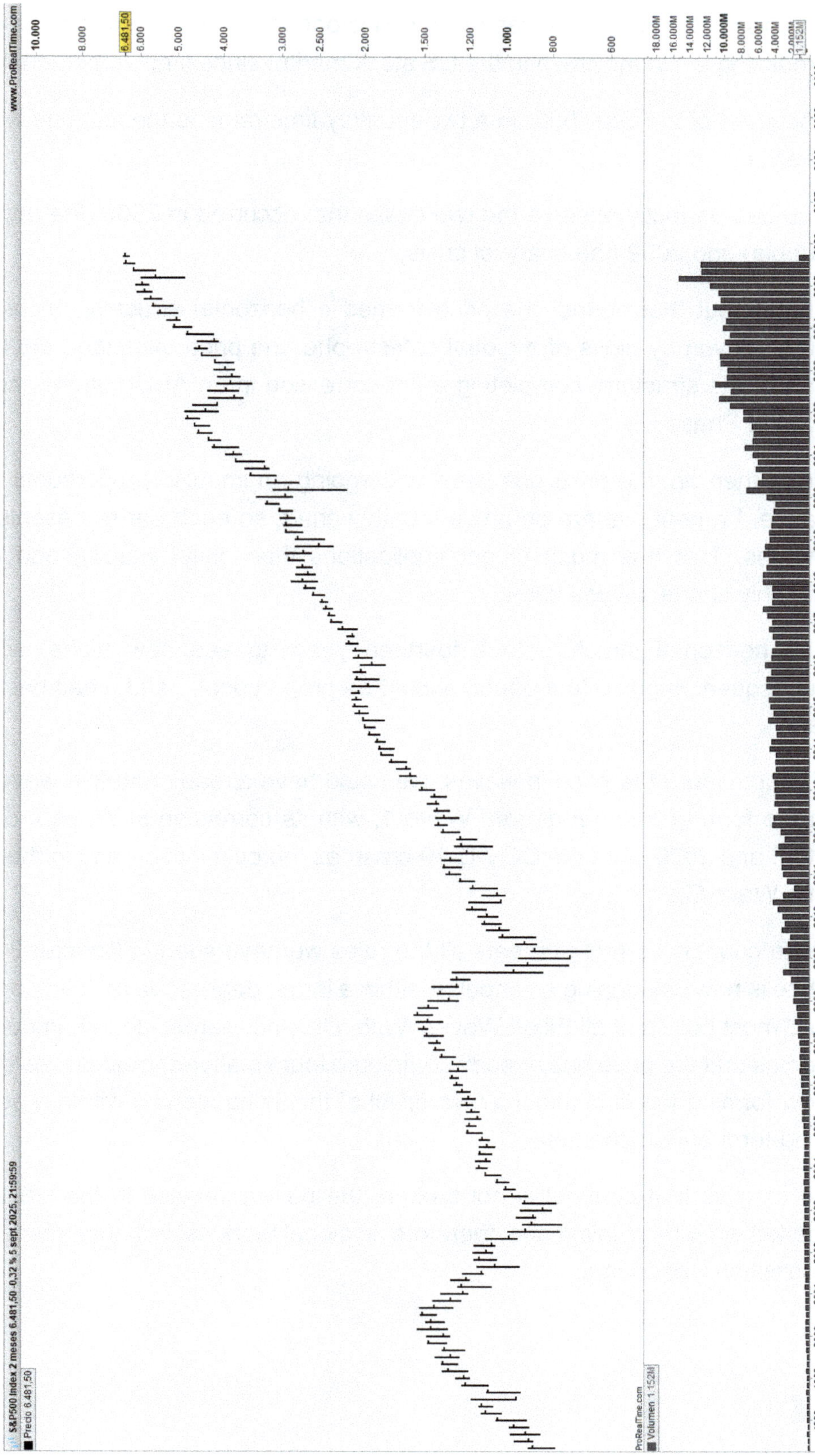

To finish, here is one last case study. This one is for all those who have been predicting a historic crash in the US stock market since time immemorial.

The chart of the S&P 500 on a two-monthly timeframe is the last one we will analyse.

You can perfectly observe the two crises that occurred in 2000 (the dot-com bubble) and 2009 (the financial crisis).

Throughout that period, the price formed a horizontal structure. In fact, in 2009, driven by news of a global catastrophe, the price expanded the lower part of the structure, completing a flat correction in an ABC pattern and the TSO of Phase C.

From then on, the price has been undergoing an impulse proportional to its cause. I repeat, we are on a two-monthly chart, so each bar represents two months. This has much bigger implications than daily, weekly, and even monthly charts, as you know.

The horizontal structure took fourteen years to see new highs, so the subsequent impulse (the effect) should be proportional... and it has been, so far.

If we structure the price in waves, we could have already had five waves up in the form of a larger-degree Wave 1, with its correction in Wave 2 during 2018 and 2020 (with the COVID-19 crash as the culmination and in the form of a Wave C).

If the count is correct (it meets all the rules we have seen in Chapter 3), the price is now developing an impulse within a larger degree Wave 3, the longest and most bullish of all Elliott Waves. Within this new larger-degree impulse, it seems that the price has already completed four smaller-degree waves and is now forming the final minor Wave 5. All of this is happening within a perfect long-term bullish channel.

As long as that channel is not broken, the bullish impulse in the US stock market will remain intact and, therefore, in global markets, with their respective corrections, of course.

Case 20: SP500 (Solution)

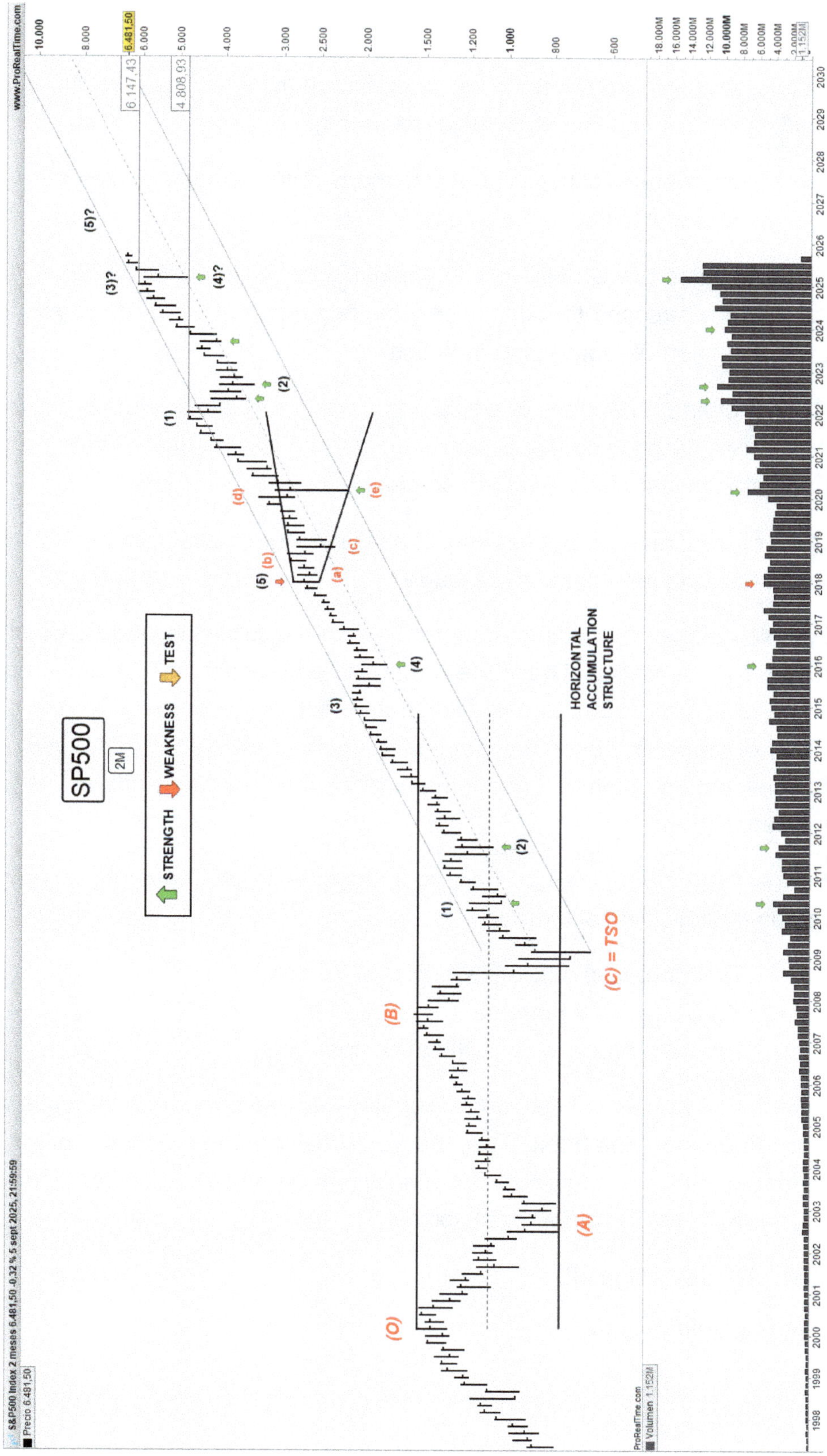

At this point, all that's left for me to do is congratulate you—you've finished reading a book that I've really enjoyed writing.

We've covered a lot of theory, but also many practical case studies that I hope will prove useful to you in the future.

All that's left is to wish you luck in this business, which is full of deadly traps. I've already stressed that this is only the beginning. It's now up to you to put everything you've learned into practice.

Charts, charts, and more charts are the answer to everything. With practice and by revisiting the concepts explained in this book, you'll be able to gradually understand what you see on the screen.

Can you confirm now that this way of analysing the market through VSA is like understanding the market's language?

I've also included a bibliography for you on the following pages, which you might find interesting. These are the books and resources I consulted online while writing this book to help "focus the shot" on what I was writing about. Many of them have been mentioned throughout this journey and a few others haven't, but I recommend reading all of them and the many others I've surely missed.

Furthermore, if you'd like to share your thoughts on VSA with me, you can find me on the following platforms:

- Twitter (social network X): @RA8Finance
- YouTube: RA8 Finance
- Website: https://www.ra8finance.com/

In fact, on those social networks, I regularly upload charts like the ones we've seen throughout the book. Also, the YouTube channel has numerous videos of market analysis applying VSA. Finally, on the website, you can find all the charts from the book in a digital format.

With all that, I'll sign off.

See you in the markets!

BIBLIOGRAPHY

- Cagigas, Ó. G. (2010). Modern theory and practice of Elliott waves.
- Holmes, G. (2011). Trading in the shadow of smart money.
- VSA Mentorship. (2023). Personal notes from the J.A. Herrera Mentorship.
- Ramírez, M. Á. (2019). Price and volume (following in the professional's footsteps).
- Williams, T. (2005). Master the markets.
- Wyckoff Analytics: https://www.wyckoffanalytics.com/

www.ingramcontent.com/pod-product-compliance
Lightning Source LLC
Chambersburg PA
CBHW061355240926
51846CB00007B/1419
9788409767403